OVERCOMING DEPRESSION
A Personal Journey

Chris Lewis

Table of Contents

Introduction

This is not a how-to book.

This book is about my personal journey with depression and the lessons I have learned from it. I hope that some of the lessons I have learned might help you too, but I learned a long time ago that there is no such thing as *Four Easy Steps to Overcoming Depression.*

I invite you, however, to join me in my journey. If you suffer from depression, I sincerely hope that my story might give you some hope and that the lessons that helped me might help you too. Take what is helpful and toss aside anything that's not. After all, every journey is unique, but I do believe that we are stronger when we journey together. We are not meant to face depression alone.

If you don't suffer from depression, I invite you to please read this book in order to have a better understanding of what people you love are going through when they fight this debilitating illness. One thing that is needed is compassion and understanding from loved-ones. Perhaps my journey will help you to give a bit more compassion and understanding to someone you love.

Depression is not a rare disease. Over 300 million people worldwide suffer from it, and according to the World Health Organization it is "the leading cause of disability worldwide, and is a major contributor to the overall global burden of disease."[i]

It is, however, rarely understood. People who struggle with depression are often told to just "suck it up" and that it's "all in their heads." Some doctors don't recognize it as a genuine illness because they can't *see* it, and some employers mistake it for laziness or a bad attitude. Some evangelicals think it's a sign of "sin" and that the cure is simple repentance, while others think it should always be overcome by a simple prayer and that if you still suffer it's because of a lack of faith.

This book will deal with some of these misconceptions and seek to help people to overcome some misunderstandings. At the end of the book, I will also share some suggestions for the loved-ones of people who suffer from depression, as well as some encouragement. After all, depression is not only hard for those of us who suffer from it directly. It can also present unique challenges to those who are near and dear to us. I hope that this book will be an encouragement both to those who suffer from depression and to those who love someone who suffers from it.

Depression is an illness. It is as real as a broken leg. However, it is not a hopeless illness, even though we may feel like it when we are in the middle of it. It can't necessarily be cured. Some people suffer from it for life. However, it can be treated and helped, and it is possible for someone who has it to go on to live a productive and good life.

At least that's my experience. I invite you to join me in my journey.

PART 1 -
My Journey

Chapter 1
Seeds of Depression

My journey with depression probably started in my childhood, though I didn't realize it at the time. I always struggled with a bit of what you might call "melancholy." I was raised in a family of entertainers, and I was involved in entertainment from the age of 6. I got used to being in front of large crowds, TV cameras and recording studio microphones very early, and I quickly learned the value of "image." I was considered by some at the time to be a "little boy wonder" and always had the pressure to maintain that image. I'm not sure I was really that good. I just had the "cute" factor, but it was an interesting childhood all the same.

I don't think that made me feel depressed though. I enjoyed it. What it did do, however, was influence my very first coping mechanism. One of my two favorite songs was an old Nat King Cole song called, "Pretend." The lyrics start out with these words:

> *Pretend you're happy when you're blue*
> *It isn't very hard to do*
> *And you'll find happiness without an end*
> *Whenever you pretend[ii]*

My other favorite song at the time was another old song that had also been recorded by Nat King Cole. It was called "Smile." Here is a sample of its lyrics:

> *Smile tho' your heart is aching*
> *Smile even tho' it's breaking*
> *When there are clouds in the sky*
> *You'll get by...*
>
> *That's the time*
> *You must keep on trying*

Smile, what's the use of crying
You'll find that life is still worth-while

If you just smile[iii]

I think you probably get the idea.

The whole purpose of my young life was to put on a good show. I knew how to pretend. I did it night after night in front of the crowds, and I came to believe that if I maintained an image of happiness all would be well.

Now don't get me wrong. I wouldn't say that I was a particularly unhappy child. My severe depression hit me much later in life. However, I can certainly see early seeds of it in my secret melancholy nature as a child. I don't think that even my own family was aware of it though. I was a good showman.

I think the way I would describe my youth would be as a very happy one but with strong shades of an inner sadness that I didn't understand. I kept it bottled up behind a smile, and it didn't come unbottled until my late twenties.

I grew up in a deeply religious family. We travelled around singing "southern Gospel" music and travelled a lot with a Gospel quartet in the late 70's and early 80's called the Blackwood Brothers, as well as doing concerts together with others like the Speer Family and the Kingsmen. If you don't know who any of those people are, it's ok. They're part of a very select genre that is mostly known in the southern states. My dad was an associate producer of the Blackwood Brothers TV show, and we were regulars on it. It was a Christian musical variety program. We also recorded albums, had our own radio program for 8 years and travelled all over the USA giving concerts.

It was an unusual childhood, and I don't regret it. It was a small-time sort of "fifteen minutes of fame" that made for a very different kind of childhood. I got to meet a lot of amazing people and experienced things many people dream of all their lives. It did have a couple of downsides, though, which may have contributed toward some of my issues later in life.

One of the downsides was that my social development got off to a slow start. I knew how to come alive in front of a crowd of 5,000 people and was perfectly comfortable on stage, but I didn't know how to interact personally with kids my own age.

I was taken out of school in the middle of third grade because I was away too much to keep up. I was enrolled in a correspondence school based out of Baltimore, Maryland. It was a very structured course with regular exams, and I learned a lot. In fact, I discovered that academically it was more advanced than many primary schools, and I excelled in my studies. However, I studied alone, getting help from my parents when I had questions, so I didn't have any friends my own age.

I still have clear memories of sitting in the lounge area at a TV studio in South Bend, Indiana doing my school work in between takes. I would study for awhile, be called in to the studio to film, and then go back to the sofa out front and continue with my schooling. I actually enjoyed that set-up immensely, but I know now that I was missing out on a normal social development.

I didn't get to know anyone my own age until I was 15. At this point, my sisters, my brother and I all felt that we needed to do something about the fact that we didn't know anyone our own ages, so we started going to the youth group at a local church. Over the next few years, I made several friends, though I don't really feel I caught up socially until I was in my early twenties. As a result, I always felt a little bit like an "outsider" on the social scene. In fact, I didn't fully get over my "outsider" feeling until I was 29. We'll get to that in the another chapter though.

The other downside was the obsession with "image." My family was pretty well-known in my hometown, and my dad was always insistent that the kids always needed to guard the family image carefully. He didn't want anyone to ever see us arguing or getting into trouble of any kind.

Ironically, we didn't tend to get into much trouble anyhow. We were pretty good kids, to be honest, but there was that constant pressure, and I am pretty sure that the sense that I had to "look" good played a big part in decisions I made later regarding my fight with depression.

So, to sum up, the main seeds I can see in my childhood that I believe played a part in my later journey with depression were these:

1) A secret, melancholy spirit that I never told anyone about
2) A lack of friends in childhood that led to my feelings of being an "outsider" in the normal world
3) A pressure to always put on a "show" and maintain a good image which caused me to hide my struggle behind a smile

Now don't get me wrong. Overall, mine actually was a very happy childhood, but these issues were definitely present even if I wasn't fully aware of them at the time. Their effect would not be understood, though, until much later.

Chapter 2
The Guilt Cycle Begins

I messed up.

I took a test for something, and I panicked and cheated. I had never done this before in my life, and I felt horrible.

It wasn't a university exam or anything like that, but it was a course I had taken on a specific subject that interested me, and I felt I had cheated myself by copying answers from the answer sheet which I happened to have access to. I also felt like the certificate I got was then a fraud.

I was 29 years old, and this was just before I went on vacation with my brother to New York City. I didn't want a test hanging over my head while on vacation, so I rushed it beforehand to get it out of the way. And I panicked.

This was hanging over me during my first 2 days of vacation and made it really difficult to enjoy myself. After a couple of days, I called my examiner and confessed. He told me not to worry about it this once. I had taken a lot of exams on this course legitimately, and they knew I was a good student and that I knew my stuff. I was forgiven.

But I still felt guilty.

Now I felt like I had ruined the first two days of this vacation I had been looking forward to for so long by obsessing over my feelings of guilt, so I spent the third day feeling guilty for having felt guilty. The next day, I felt like I had already ruined half of my vacation by obsessing over guilt feelings, so I felt guilty for that.

And the cycle continued.

For the next ten years, the guilt cycle became my constant companion. I would go through times in which it would leave me alone, but pretty much any time I had a day off, a vacation, or any experience that I felt should be relaxing or enjoyable, I spent much of that time feeling guilty...

....and then feeling guilty for feeling guilty...

...and then feeling guilty for that.

A few months after that New York vacation, I moved to Scotland and started a college course there. I was in Scotland for a year before going back temporarily to the USA, and during that time the guilt cycle was intense. I kept going through this general cycle of guilt, and on top of that I could never quite get that test I'd taken out of my head.

When I returned to the USA for a short time after my first year in Scotland, I had another talk with the man who had given me that exam. I told him how I had been feeling, and he reassured me that I really needed to let that go. I had confessed my one failure very quickly after I had done it, my confession had been taken account of, and I had been completely forgiven. I needed to forgive myself.

And I did. I forgave myself for that error and never let it bother me again.

Except...

Except that I now felt like I had ruined an otherwise wonderful year by obsessing over guilt feelings I didn't need to worry so much about....

And the cycle continued.

I didn't know it then, but guilt feelings are a classic symptom of chronic depression. I have since talked to many people who struggle, and most of them have told me that they can identify with this part of my story. Something within us becomes convinced that we are to blame for our depression, and we often find ourselves blaming ourselves and feeling guilty for all kinds of things.

I had a lot of talks with people who were close to me, and sometimes I think they must have thought I was going crazy. In my case, I became particularly concerned with the idea of "ruining my day." I would ask the few people I confided in, "Have I ruined my day?" By indulging in self-pity and feelings of guilt, I would look at the positive things I was experiencing in life and convince myself that I had ruined them because I thought I "should" enjoy them but felt that I was not capable of enjoying them as much as I should have because of my guilt.

When I think of some of the thought patterns that tortured me during that time now, I can see that they really were irrational. However, when I was in the midst of it I couldn't see it. All I could see was my guilt.

It consumed me, off and on, for about ten years. I would have periods of time in which it didn't bother me as much, but it was always there. The more I enjoyed life, the more I worried that I wasn't enjoying it enough! You'd think my mind would have chosen something else to obsess over, but I sincerely felt like whenever I had an opportunity to enjoy a vacation, a day off, or a good moment I was ruining it if I spent any of that time worrying about something or feeling depressed. Then after feeling guilty about it, I would talk to someone who would help me to see again that I didn't need to feel guilty about being depressed, but I would then feel like I ruined my day by feeling guilty needlessly.

And so I would feel guilty about that.

The depressed mind is often like a torture chamber in which we are both the torturer and the tortured. Irrational thoughts flood our minds and take control, and even if we eventually come to realize that they are irrational we become inwardly addicted to those thoughts and find it incredibly difficult to break free.

When I was a child, my family had a dog named Bandit who always walked the exact same paths around the land behind our house. Because he always walked back and forth along the same route, a path was created in which the grass never grew. Even if we went on vacation for a month and came back to find the surrounding land had turned into a jungle, Bandit's rut would remain untouched by the grass.

Our minds tend to become like Bandit's ruts. We create neural pathways with our repetitive thinking. Our minds walk back and forth along the same path for so long that ruts are created in which no grass grows, no new life blooms, and no logic penetrates. No matter how hard we try to create new paths, our thinking keeps falling back into the same old ruts.

This is what happened to me. My guilt became Bandit's ruts, and it was incredibly difficult to get out of them! In time, I learned to create new pathways and to follow them, but it took time. To start with, I would learn to turn my mind down a new path, and it would work for awhile. But then the smallest thing would pull me right back into the old familiar rut.

Once these ruts become a part of us, it takes time and effort, and we find that creating new pathways for our minds to travel is not something we can do alone. It took me ten years to become comfortable walking different pathways in my thinking and for the grass to finally grow along the old ones.

However, I've finally reached the point where I only occasionally visit the old paths, and I've found better ones to travel. I got worse before I got better though, as you will see in the next chapter.

Chapter 3
The Storm Hits

"It was the best of times, it was the worst of times."[iv] Thus wrote my favorite classic author, Charles Dickens, in the opening of one of his greatest works, and these words aptly describe my college years in Scotland. Overall, I would actually say they were some of the happiest years of my life. They were, however, also the years in which I first realized I had a problem with depression.

In college, I was mostly happy. I found a group of friends, and we hung out all the time. We would sometimes cook dinners at each others' houses, or go to the live jazz nights on Fridays at the coffee shop in the Borders bookstore, or just hang out. We'd sometimes study together when exams were near, and we even travelled together for vacation. This was a great experience for me because it was the first time in my life I didn't feel at all like an outsider. And after that, I never did feel like an outsider again. I finally felt like I had caught up socially.

I'll never forget my 30th birthday. When it was time for a break between classes, I went to the common room in the college, and my fellow students had decorated it with balloons and banners. They yelled surprise, gave me a birthday cake, and made me feel truly loved and appreciated.

However, though much of the time I was actually very happy, I found that my "bad days" were increasingly worse as well. I would have days in which I felt utterly depressed, and I didn't know what was happening to me.

For several years before that, I had struggled with what I considered to be my "bad days," but I had not yet recognized them as signs of a serious problem. I would have days when I would feel a heaviness upon me that I couldn't explain. This would last for a few days and then it would suddenly lift and I would feel really happy again. They weren't debilitating, but looking back I recognize them now as a precursor of what was to come.

I was really fortunate that the period of time in which I began to experience a deeper struggle was also at a time time when I was surrounded consistently by good friends. There was one friend in particular, whom I will just refer to as R., who was especially helpful. Her dad also struggled with depression, so she recognized the signs and was the first person to talk to me about it. She helped me to see that I was dealing with depression, and at this phase in my life she could always talk me through it. After a good chat with her, I wouldn't feel depressed again for awhile, and during my college days I learned that any time it got on top of me a chat with my friend would help to lift me back up.

Now if you are reading this and thinking, "But that's not real depression! Nobody can talk you out of depression when it hits!" my response to that is that I know that now. The day would come when nobody could talk me through, talk me out or talk me down. However, at this phase of my journey it was still possible 90 percent of the time for me to talk through what I was thinking with someone who understood and could help me to sort through my feelings and come out feeling better for awhile. This friend, in particular, had a good understanding of what I was going through and could always help me. She was also the first person to help me see and begin to accept that it was a form of depression. Before that time, I would always have denied that I had depression, but at this point in my life I began to recognize it for what it was, at least to an extent. I did, however, convince myself by the time my college years were over that I had completely overcome my depression and would never be depressed again.

I could not have been more wrong about that.

The big storm hit me a few months after I graduated from college.

The year was 2005. I had graduated from my college course in the summer, and I was working for a local church near Glasgow. Things had gone really well.

The people at the church seemed great, and I enjoyed my job.

I had fallen in love.

Life was good.

That summer I went on vacation by myself in Egypt and had the most enjoyable trip I had experienced in years. For the first time in four years, I did not struggle with the guilt cycle or depression. I relaxed, I had fun, I met a lot of great people, and I saw a lot of fascinating sites.

Then in August, after a trip to East Africa working with the poor in Tanzania, I came back to Scotland.

Several key people in the church turned against me.

The girl I thought I loved rejected me.

And I fell into a deep and painful depression.

When I was younger, I did not understand why anybody would consider suicide. In my mind, it was simply not an option, and I had looked down a bit on anybody who would consider it. It just seemed wrong.

Now it felt like an option. There was such a heaviness upon me, and such a sense of complete and utter despair, that I felt like I simply could not go on. After that, I would never look down upon anybody who was considering suicide. I understood.

Fortunately, though, there was an older man I had gotten to know who understood about depression. He and his wife were very good to me, and they helped me to come to terms with what was happening to me.

During my college years, I had come to terms with the idea that I had depression to a certain extent, but I still had been careful not to let many people know. I felt like there was a stigma attached to it, and the old feeling that I had to maintain a certain image still hung on.

However, this man, whose name was Bill, helped me to understand that it was not something to be ashamed of. He explained to me that it was an illness, just like any other illness. A lot of people couldn't understand it because they couldn't *see* it, but he said that regardless of whether people could see it or not, it was just as real as a broken leg.

Bill arranged for me to visit a local doctor to talk about my situation, so I went to the doctor and told him all about what I was feeling. He recognized that I was depressed, so he picked up a piece of script for prescriptions and wrote a prescription for me. This is what he wrote:

"See it through bravely."

I read his *prescription*, and I wanted to die. He explained to me that it was all in my head and that I just needed to learn to think differently, to be courageous and work through it. Then I would be fine.

I knew, however, that I could not see it through bravely. I felt at that moment that if this was the best anyone could offer me, there was truly no hope.

When I went back and told Bill what the doctor had said, he was mortified and, I think, a little angry. He explained to me that some doctors have a blind spot when it comes to depression and just don't understand it. This doctor may have been good when treating other things, but in this particular case he was simply wrong.

Bill gave me some literature that helped me to understand depression a little better. He was a pharmacist and had some training on the medical side of the issue as well as personal experience in supporting friends and family members who struggled personally with the disease. According to him there are basically two kinds of depression. He said, "There are two general types of depression. One is situational: it is caused by something you go through in life. It is usually temporary and may go away and never come back after you have dealt with the situation. The other is chronic: it's an illness as real as a broken leg, and it doesn't go away. However, there is hope and there is help available."

With his help, I did get a prescription for an anti-depressant, though obviously not from the same doctor. Getting me to accept it without shame, though, was another challenge.

To be honest, at first I didn't feel any shame. I only felt desperation. I felt convinced that if something didn't help me soon I simply and literally could not go on. So at the beginning at least I accepted the medication gladly, though not without fear.

I didn't know if it would work, but I was willing to give it a try.

During the first few days, I didn't feel better. I felt worse. However, Bill had warned me that it could take a couple of weeks before I would feel the benefit. As my anxiety worsened, he explained that it was probably a side effect and that usually most side-effects would disappear by the end of two weeks. I hoped this was true, but I would believe it when I saw it.

Another side-effect I experienced was trembling in my legs. My legs would start shaking and wouldn't stop for awhile. It was really scary, especially for someone who was already struggling with anxiety!

Fortunately, though, the side-effects in my case did wear off, and after a couple of weeks I started feeling better. I was able to cope again, though I still struggled with a lot of mixed up thinking and the guilt cycle continued for years. Taking an anti-depressant did not cure me, but it was a step in the direction toward having hope again.

Getting over the "stigma" was difficult for me though. What helped me was that a couple of other people with depression talked with me and shared their experiences with me. One friend said she had been taking anti-depressants for years. She had tried coming off them a year or so before that and had slipped back into severe depression, so she had started taking them again and was doing pretty well. She was running a successful business and doing really well in life. It gave me hope.

My friends who had suffered with depression, as well as my pharmacist friend, also talked to me about the myth that "anti-depressants will dampen your personality." I was scared to death that the medications would change my personality drastically, and I didn't want that! They all explained to me, however, that the aim of the medication was to help get the levels of serotonin, a natural chemical in my body, to the level they are *supposed* to be in a healthy person and that the goal was not to change my personality but to help me to be free to fully be myself again.

As time has passed, I am convinced they were right. Anti-depressants have not "changed my personality." They have, instead, helped to set me free to be the person I am when I am healthy and to seek the further help that I have needed to restore myself back to better mental health.

Of course, I also learned that anti-depressants are not a "cure-all." I think at first I hoped that once the medications did their job I wouldn't ever be depressed again. That, of course, led to some disappointments and further lessons to be learned.

I started taking anti-depressants in December of 2005. Then I spent a month in Nicaragua in January. It was a wonderful month. I stayed on an island in the middle of a large saltwater lake with good friends on their organic farm. For four wonderful weeks I lived in a tropical paradise, relaxing in a hammock, hiking through the rainforest, watching movies, eating ad talking with my good friends, and reading a lot of books. It was heaven....almost.

However, I did discover that I still wasn't in the clear. My old friend, Mr. Guilt, was still with me.

My first day or two in Nicaragua were extremely peaceful, but then on the third day I started feeling guilty about something. I don't even remember what it was, but after a day or so of the guilt I realized I was feeling guilty for no good reason. But was that the end of it? Of course not! Now I felt like I had already ruined one day of my retreat by feeling guilty, so I followed up by feeling guilty for feeling guilty, and then feeling guilty for feeling guilty for feeling guilty.

I did not struggle every day while I was in Nicaragua, but I had some days in which I most definitely did. I also had some days in which I felt the old heaviness return. I did not feel anything close to suicidal any more, but there were days in which I most definitely did feel depressed. I didn't understand. I had hoped the anti-depressant would be a magical pill. But of course it wasn't!

Over the next year, the idea of counselling was mentioned to me more than once, but I didn't like the idea. Now that I was finally getting over my perceived stigma about medication, I still had negative ideas about counselling. I thought it was a good idea for other people, but I still felt like it would be admitting that something was wrong with me or something. In the back of my head, I knew I needed help, but I couldn't get myself to accept it.

A year or so later, it was decided that maybe I was taking the wrong medication, so we toyed around with two or three different ones over the next year or two. One definitely seemed to make me feel worse, another one better, but of course no medication could totally cure me. I didn't understand that yet, but depression was not something you could just get rid of with a magical pill. There was still a lot I had to learn!

Chapter 4
Overcoming the Stigma of Counselling

My attitude about counselling was strange. I often recommended it to other people and even received some training in the field of counselling in college, but for a long time I couldn't talk myself into it. I would tell people, "There's nothing to be ashamed of. Everybody needs help sometimes, and there's no reason to feel bad about it."

But something within me still felt ashamed. I didn't want to admit I needed help. I suppose the old "Image is everything" of my childhood was still there somewhere, and somehow I felt like going to counselling would present a bad image. I don't know if that was it, but I think it must have been part of it at least. In my mind, there was a stigma attached to counselling, even though I kept arguing with myself and others that there wasn't.

I did finally decide to give it a try though. I think it was in 2007. My work in Scotland had someone they recommended over in Northern Ireland and offered to pay for my initial sessions with him, so I flew over to Belfast and met a very nice man with whom I had a great talk. I shared my whole story with him, and he listened and gave some advice.

However, I quickly realized I could predict nearly everything he was going to tell me before he opened his mouth. I had received a certain amount of counsellor training myself, and the level of knowledge I had seemed to be a hindrance to me because everything he said to me, as well as every question he asked, was exactly what I would have said or asked of someone else. So rightly or wrongly, I decided not to continue with him. I really liked him as a person, but I didn't feel he could help me.

Now was I right in that conclusion? Probably not. There was probably some truth in my thought that a fully qualified psychologist might help me more and that higher qualifications might have given me more confidence. However, I suspect that if I had continued with this man over a period of time he would have been able to help me some. I don't know for sure, but I strongly suspect that my own reluctance to get counselling was still pulling me back.

Whatever the case, my first counselling experience led nowhere.

I would strongly recommend now to anyone else in the situation I was in then not to give up so quickly. Unless there is something blaringly wrong with the counsellor, don't make excuses because chances are that that is what you are really doing. Give it a few months. Then if you are absolutely certain you need a different counsellor start thinking about changing. But whatever you do, don't just give up on counselling. I believe it is essential for most people if they are going to make headway on dealing effectively with depression.

In my case, unfortunately, I didn't try counselling again for another two years. When I finally really gave counselling a chance, however, it changed my life.

The guilt-cycle was sometimes getting completely debilitating, and I also went through more periods of deep depression. I never again fell into it as deeply as I had in 2005, but it still got really bad. I finally gave in and accepted that I could not make any further progress in my journey without professional help.

I found a psychologist and began to meet with him on a weekly basis. He helped me to work through a lot of the distorted thinking patterns that I had developed and to understand more of the roots of my issues. By the end of our sessions, I had made more progress than I could ever have imagined.

And now I am left with absolutely no sense of stigma regarding counselling. I believe it can be life-changing, and honestly I suspect that everybody could benefit from it from time to time. Don't let anybody tell you that you have to be "crazy" or "sick" to go to a psychologist or psychiatrist. We all have cobwebs that build up in our minds from time to time, and it can be a very helpful experience to talk them over with someone who has a deeper understanding of the workings of the human mind than us.

I admit that the sessions weren't always comfortable, but being uncomfortable isn't always a bad thing. The most uncomfortable moment for me was when he made me have a dialogue with my right thumb.

I had been unconsciously picking my right thumb for years, and it was always injured with skin coming off, callouses, etc. He suggested that my habit had something to do with punishing myself for my guilt feelings or something like that, and he told me to have a dialogue with my thumb and have my thumb tell me how it felt being treated the way I was treating it. I tried and then said I couldn't do it.

He asked me, "Why? Are you feeling anger at me for telling you to do this? How does this make you feel?"

I said, "It just feels silly."

I did eventually learn to stop picking my thumb so much though, and though there were certainly uncomfortable moments, the counselling changed my life. The guilt issue didn't resolve itself immediately, but in time it did mostly resolve itself as a result of those sessions. I've finally been able to recognize when they start to come that they are simply a symptom of the illness and not really me, and I no longer let them control me or debilitate me. They start to come from time to time, but I no longer entertain them, and when I don't entertain them they fade to the background and become nothing more than a bit of white noise in the background that no longer controls my life.

One thing I learned though was that I couldn't simply ignore the guilt feelings. Trying not to think of something is the surest way of making sure that we do think about it! It's like if somebody tells you not to think about pink elephants, what will you start thinking about? Pink elephants of course!

In order to move the guilt feelings into the background, I had to learn to replace those thoughts with new thoughts. It's like with those ruts I talked about. I had to learn how to create new neural pathways in my brain, to create new thought patterns and train myself to think about different things. Until I learned how to think about other things rather than simply trying to *not* think about guilt, I got nowhere. Counselling helped me learn how to do this, and I honestly don't think I could have learned how to do it without help.

My dad was always very distrustful of psychologists and psychiatrists, and I suspect that his distrust of them contributed toward my fear of them as an adult and the unfortunate delay in finally giving them a chance to help me. However, the reality is that there should be no stigma attached to getting help. If you have cancer, you go to see a doctor. There's no shame in that! If you have depression or some other kind of mental illness, it's no different. The only logical thing to do is to go to the people who are trained to help. There is absolutely no shame in seeking help.

If you have considered counselling but have refused to go for one reason or another, please give it a try. Chronic depression is an illness, and I don't believe it ever simply goes away. However, there is hope of getting it under control so that it no longer controls your life. Many times a combination of medicine and counselling are the answer. In time you may even reach the point that you no longer need antidepressants, but even if you always need them it is nothing to be ashamed of. My dad had a heart condition, and he had to take medication for the rest of his life to keep it under control. The medication was successful, but nobody ever told him, "Now that you're feeling better, stop taking the meds!" To do so would probably have killed him. So if your doctors tell you that you should keep taking your medications, please keep taking them and don't ever feel ashamed of that!

However, at the same time, please remember that medications alone don't clear up the mixed up thinking patterns that are created in our brains by this illness. Counselling from a qualified professional who truly understands depression and the workings of the human brain can go a long way in helping to sort things out. It might even save your life!

Chapter 5
Overcoming: A Continuing Story

The past few years have been great! To finally not be overwhelmed by feelings of guilt and carrying a deep heaviness with me is a relief so great that it is hard to even explain. That doesn't mean that I am cured though. It just means that the illness is under control.

I still have bad days, but lately I've been able to recognize them for what they are and sort of "ride them out" with the knowledge and understanding that I will feel better the next day. A few areas where I still struggle, however, are:

A) Approval Addiction

I really want people to like me, and I have to confess that when people don't it hurts me deeper than it does some people. If somebody gets angry with me or turns against me, I still fall into a deep depression. In the past, it would effect me for a very long time and add an extra layer to my depression. The good news is that in the past few years the depression I feel when that happens only lasts for a little while. In fact, usually I will have one day, or in extreme cases a few days, of being incredibly down. Then the next day, I accept the new reality and begin to move on.

There are a few theories as to why I am that way. According the Meyers-Briggs personality tests, I am an ENFP, and I've been told that it is natural for my personality type to struggle a little extra with approval addiction. However, I suspect that the expectations put upon me in my childhood to always put on a good show and to maintain the right "image" could have a lingering influence upon me as well.

This doesn't affect me nearly as badly as it used to though. In the past, if I thought somebody didn't like me I would go into a deep depression for quite some time. There was a couple in Scotland with whom I was very close who one day completely turned on me, and it really crushed me for awhile. It wasn't until I went to counselling that I eventually began to come to terms with it, whereas another colleague turned upon me pretty drastically earlier this year and it only affected me deeply for a few days before I started to come to terms with the new reality and move on accordingly. Of course, there will still be a random day in which my mind starts going over the hurt I've experienced and it might get me down again for a few hours, but none of it effects me as deeply as it used to.

All the same, I am still to sensitive to criticism. For example, if this book gets a bad review on Amazon, I can pretty much guarantee you that I will get depressed over it for a day! However, by the next day I will have accepted it and moved on.

One sign that I am not as bad in this area as I used to be is how I respond to the horrible and hateful messages I receive almost daily on Twitter. Even as recently as a year ago, I always regretted it if I got into a debate about politics or some other subject on Facebook or in person because when people started belittling me or insulting me I would get really depressed about it. Now, however, some comments occasionally sting, but most of the time I just brush them off. The block button also comes in handy of course!

B) Excessive time-consciousness

This may never happen to you, but this is a way in which the perfectionism and work-ethic of my father has manifested itself in me. I am incredibly conscious of how I use my time, and I worry more than necessary about "wasting time." If I feel that I have not used my time wisely in a day, sometimes I let it get me down for a whole day, and I know that my sense of what it means to "use my time well" isn't always logical.

For example, if I'm working I may stress about whether I "accomplished enough" that day even when nobody else cares and everybody is happy with what I've accomplished. And if it is a day off, I tend to obsess about whether I've chosen my activities well in such a way as to maximize my enjoyment...and in doing so I can sometimes minimize my enjoyment in the process!

This also isn't nearly as bad as it used to be though. In the past, it was often the trigger that led me into a fresh guilt cycle. If I felt that I hadn't used my time well, I would begin to think I had "wasted my day." Then I would spend all day the following day feeling guilty for having wasted the day before, then the next day feeling guilty that I had wasted a day in feeling guilty and so on as the guilt cycle snowballed once again.

Thankfully I don't do that anymore, so there is hope that I will continue to improve in this area as well.

However, I share these examples of areas in which I still struggle in order to make what I believe is a very important point:

Overcoming depression is a journey, and we are all in different phases of our journey. This journey is one that is always moving forward, though, not backwards.

You might be where I was in chapter 2 or 3, or you might be exactly where I am. Wherever you are, that's ok. It's a journey, and there continues to be hope.

I am also realistic enough about my illness to know that I can't guarantee I won't have more very difficult seasons in the future. I hope that I never go back to that place where I was literally despairing of life itself, but I can't guarantee it. I do choose, however, not to dwell on those possibilities but to focus on the present. I have learned, for me at least, that one of the most important things I can do is to live in the present as much as possible, to make the best of today. Tomorrow will come when it comes, and I can hope and dream and plan, but there is no value in excessively worrying about problems that may never come. And there is absolutely no value in focusing on regrets. The past is gone, but today we have an opportunity to start fresh. My life will never move backwards, so there is no help found in focusing too much energy on the past. I am moving forward.

You may not be to the point where you can accept these thoughts yet. You might be in the midst of a deep and painful depressive season. However, I can say that I've been where you are and found light at the end of the tunnel even though at the time I did not believe that would ever be possible.

Keep moving forward. There is hope ahead.

PART 2 -

My Heart Sings: my journey through poetry

Chapter 6
Poetry

In this section, I'd like to share a short snapshot of my journey in poetic form. Several of the poems are written in free verse style, while others rhyme. Most of these poems I have written especially for this book, but a few of them were written 17 years ago during a time in which I was writing about my journey up to that time. I have made a note at the bottom of each of the ones I wrote in the past so that you will know which ones they are.

The Sunglass Kid

There was a little boy in sunglasses
Standing on the big bright stage
He sang his heart out
As the spotlight shone on his face

The show must go on
Was the motto of his life
A smile must be remain
Whether happy or in strife

Though he was a truly joyful child
The world did not yet know
That in his heart was a sadful seed
That in adulthood would one day grow

Look closer at the people you meet
You never know what is hidden
Behind the sunglasses

The Window in My Soul

Smiling faces
Often hide an empty heart
And I ought to know
For I've often hidden mine
Sometimes we say we want to be
A light unto the world
But if we have no light inside
How can we let it shine?

Where is the answer?
Where is the rock that I can stand on?
When it seems that all around me
Just blows right through my soul
Where is the answer?
What can fill this void inside me?
As the wind just keeps on blowing
Through the window in my soul

It seems I've spent a lifetime
Grasping at the wind
I want to hold it in my hand
But I cannot understand
The wind just keeps on blowing,
Blowing right through me
As my feet are planted solidly
On a rock of shifting sand

Where is the answer?
Where is the rock that I can stand on?
When it seems that all around me
Just blows right through my soul
Where is the answer?
What can fill this void inside me?
As the wind just keeps on blowing
Through the window in my soul

- written on January 4, 2000

Guilty

Someone told me there was no condemnation
But there certainly was a lot of it
Inside my head

A judge proclaimed me guilty
And made a big long list
Inside my head

I realised the judge was me
And I was wrong
Inside my head

But then I felt guilty
For listening to the voice
Inside my head

And so a battle raged
Between the judge
And the judged
Who both were me

And a vicious cycle
That would not stop
Nearly drove me mad
As the judge's gavel

Grew louder

And stronger

Inside my head

The Fugitive

I'm a fugitive
And I'm running all the time
I wear a different mask each day
Hoping no one will see inside

I ran across the ocean
And I ran across the land
I tried to find a shelter
But there was no place to hide

If there's an answer
It's not in me
Why am I running?
Why can't I see?

Some people tell me
Just look inside
But that's where I see that
I'm trying to hide

My greatest enemy
Is inside of me
And I need someone
To set me free

I'm a fugitive

I ran from my pursuer
And I found a place to hide
But then I looked into the mirror
And I saw his face inside

He keeps on following me
Where can I go?
Is there a hiding place?
I need to know

Won't someone help me?
Won't someone try
Won't someone listen
To my feeble cry?
Won't someone hear me
And tell me why
Won't someone help me
Before I die?

> If there's an answer
> It's not in me
> Why am I running?
> Why can't I see?

> Some people tell me
> Just look inside
> But that's where I see that
> I'm trying to hide

> My greatest enemy
> Is inside of me
> And I need someone
> To set me free

> I'm a fugitive

I keep on running
But I don't know where
And wherever I wander
I can feel his stare

Won't someone help me?
Won't someone try
Won't someone listen
To my feeble cry?
Won't someone hear me
And tell me why
Won't someone help me
Before I die?

> If there's an answer
> It's not in me
> Why am I running?
> Why can't I see?

> Some people tell me
> Just look inside
> But that's where I see that
> I'm trying to hide

> My greatest enemy
> Is inside of me
> And I need someone
> To set me free

> I'm a fugitive

- Written in 2000

Flower of Scotland

Flower of Scotland
You bloomed bright for me
But you were filled with poison
That I didn't immediately see

You bloomed both beautiful and dark
You revealed the darkness within me
But also set my light aflame

In you I found both my beginnings and my ends
Sadness
And joy

Oh flower of Scotland
You will always be mine
And I will always be yours

My deepest pain
And my greatest joy

Shipwreck

I looked into the water
And saw a window to my heart
I saw that it was crying
And I did not understand

I looked into the ocean
And saw a window to my soul
I saw that it was swimming
And it could not find the land

I am lost upon the ocean of a trillion tears
I am freezing in the rain of all my doubts and fears
Won't someone come and rescue me
As I shiver in the rain?
I'm a shipwreck lost in a sinking world
And it's driving me insane

- written in 2000

My Bed

I should get up
But the sheets protect me from the world
And when they're unfurled
I cannot move

They tell me to just get up
But I can
Not

It is both my haven
And my prison
My heaven
And my hell

When will my bed
Release me?

A Verse Without a Rhyme

I'm a verse without a rhyme
I'm a song without a tune
I'm a room without a window
But I hope that someday...maybe
I'll get it right

I've tried to make things right
But I always make them wrong
The nights are like a lifetime
And the days are oh so...much longer
When will I get it right?

        I keep on running
        I keep on trying
        I keep on laughing
        I keep on crying

        But when will I get it right?
        When will my song take flight?

I am a bird without a song
I am a dog without a bone
I am a poet without a poem
Won't someone come and take me...somewhere
Where I can find my way?

I am a movie without a plot
I am a fire that doesn't burn
I am a car without an engine
I wonder if I will ever...know
How to find my way.

I keep on running
I keep on trying
I keep on laughing
I keep on crying

But when will I get it right?
When will my song take flight?

-    Written in 2000

The Judge

I am the judge
And the executioner
Of my soul

Help

I believed I was weak
If I needed help
But I learned that being willing to ask
Is
a
sign
of
Strength

The Darkest Hour

They say the darkest hour means dawn
Is just in sight
But it's hard to believe
When you cannot see
Anything

But there is a light
At the end
Of this tunnel

Medication

I heard them say
It will change me
My intelligence will dim
My personality will dampen
And I will disappear
Under the haze
Of a Prozac nation

They said these things
Because they did not understand
I've finally been set free
To find the real me

I am not dampened
I am not dim
And I will not disappear

Talking to my Thumb

Hello dear thumb
I'm sorry I treated you so badly
I kept picking on you
I've been such a bully

> I forgive you,
> Though I must admit
> That you caused me great pain
> And I truly can't say
> That it was no skin off my back

I realize that now
It seems I picked on you
Because I was angry at me
And I couldn't reach my heart

> I forgive you,
> And I won't seek revenge
> I will still hold your food
> And help you find a ride
> Just next time...

> Pick on somebody your own size

My Neighbor and Me

Jesus said, "Love your neighbor as you love yourself."
The thing is, though, that I've always loved my neighbor
But I haven't always loved myself

Lord help me
To love myself
as I love my neighbor.

No Condemnation

I learned to forgive the people who hurt me
And now I've learned to forgive
Me

No condemnation now I dread
I've learned the art of forgiveness instead

Hello my soul
Neither do I condemn you
Go and sin no more

The Psychologist

Tell me, how did that make you feel?
Better, doctor
Much better

Sometimes it hurts to smile
Just like I told the dentist the other day
But now I've got good news
And you're partially to thank, I must say

Now my smile
Is real

The Rose

Recovery is like a rose
It smells like heaven
And it's beautiful
But it still has thorns

\-

PART 3 -

Lessons I've Learned Along the Way

Chapter 7
I'm Not Guilty

One of the most helpful lessons I have learned is that guilt feelings are quite literally a symptom of the illness. Just because we feel guilty, it doesn't mean we're guilty.

I recently had an operation for an inguinal hernia on my left side. It was a big and direct abdominal hernia, and it was really painful. I had severe pain in my side that resonated also to my back, and it was really difficult to walk. The pain and the difficulty in walking were symptoms of my illness. They were easy to identify as such because doctors could see my hernia bulging, and we have all been well trained in life to recognize that physical pain points to a physical problem.

Many of us haven't been so well trained when it comes to emotional pain, however. When we experience emotional pain, we may tend to automatically assume either that somebody else has done something to hurt us or that we have done something to ourselves for which we should feel guilty.

But this is not always true. Emotional pain is sometimes a warning sign that there is an emotional problem that needs attention!

I have come to understand that there are basically two kinds of guilt: true guilt & false guilt

1) True guilt

Let's talk about true guilt first. I do believe that there is such a thing as real guilt, and we don't do ourselves any favors by ignoring that. If your first reaction is to say this is not true, consider some extreme examples with me for a moment.

Can we say that a rapist, a pedophile or a murderer has no guilt? Of course not! And people who commit these crimes are usually found guilty by a court of law and must face the consequences of their actions.

On the less extreme side of things, we may experience true guilt if we lie to somebody, cheat somebody or do something that causes them harm. If our conscience is at all healthy, we tend to feel guilty when we do something that is wrong.

Now this is more complicated than it seems because it does beg the question of what is right and what is wrong. There are a lot of things that we might put within what we call a *grey area*. These are things that are highly dependent upon what ethical code an individual lives by. For example, a teetotaler evangelical in the USA will probably feel guilty if he drinks one beer, a Northern Irish Christian might feel guilty if she goes shopping or eats at a restaurant on a Sunday, a Muslim or Orthodox Jew will likely feel guilty if he eats pork, and a vegetarian will feel guilty if she eats a steak. Are these things wrong? The answer in these cases is debatable and depends on your worldview and belief system.

However, without going into deep philosophical discussions about where the line is between right and wrong, I think most of us are inherently aware that there are at least some things that are simply *wrong* and for which feeling guilt is right and appropriate.

However, *true guilt does not need to last forever.*

I believe that guilt functions emotionally in much the same way the pain receptors do physically. Pain is very important because it warns of you of potential problems. For example, someone who feels no pain could put his hand in a fire or on a hot stove without ever realizing there was a problem until his hand was burnt and destroyed. *Pain is an indicator that something needs to be done to deal with a problem. The same is true with guilt.*

If I have done something that has brought harm to others, my conscience warns me that I am guilty. The purpose of guilt is not to torture me but to warn me that something needs to be done about a situation. I may need to apologize to whoever I have hurt, or sometimes I may need to make reparations or correct a situation. In the case of a crime, I may also have to face consequences of some kind or another.

However, once I have dealt with the situation, there is no longer any reason to continue to carry a burden of guilt.

Let me give some simple examples from everyday life. Let's say you have lied to your best friend and she finds out. This can have a serious effect upon your relationship. You will need to apologize and maybe talk things through with your friend. Whether or not she forgives you is up to her, but you have to forgive yourself. Once you've done all you can do to apologize and rectify a situation when you are in the wrong, there is no reason to carry a burden of guilt.

Now let's consider a situation a little more extreme. Let's say you've been stealing money from your employer. He finds out, and he's angry. Do you have a reason to feel guilty? Of course you do. You may have done what you did out of desperation because you couldn't pay the medical bills for your sick child, but whatever the justification you have done something wrong. You need to apologize, and you will almost certainly experience consequences. You might get fired from your job. You might even face jail-time depending on how extreme the situation is and whether or not your employer chooses to press charges. However, once the situation is dealt with you don't have to feel guilty about it for the rest of your life.

Of course, it's easier said that done. Sometimes people carry around guilt for things they have done for the rest of their lives. However, I do believe that true guilt ends once we have confessed our wrongdoing, accepted the consequences and done anything within our power to right our wrongs. The guilt feelings that may remain after that are what I refer to as false guilt.

2) False guilt

False guilt is that existential feeling of guilt that follows us long after we've dealt with the problem. It is also sometimes a feeling of guilt we have when we haven't actually even done anything wrong.

I'm going to suggest something to you that you may or may not accept but which I believe could have a powerful affect upon your life if you do accept it:

Guilt is not inherent to your identity.

Guilt is something that maybe from time to time you have, but it is not *who* you are.

I honestly don't believe that there is any healthy reason why a person should carry a burden of guilt with him all his life. Have you messed up? Of course you have! We all have! But if we all carried around a bag of guilt for every wrong thing we've done in life, we would all be a miserable bunch of people!

Think of guilt as an emotional pain receptor. When you feel guilty, can you point to something you have done that is objectively wrong and harmful to others? If so, go and make it right to the best of your ability. Then let it go.

If you can't let the guilt go, get counselling and work through it together with your counsellor. But refuse to let guilt define you.

I think that almost everybody struggles with some false guilt in life. When we have done something that really hurt someone we love or destroyed a marriage or damaged a family, it is natural to feel guilty. However, we shouldn't feel guilty forever. We need to deal with the consequences of things sometimes, but then we need to move on. It is essential to our mental health.

That being said, when we struggle with depression our tendency is to magnify our guilt feelings rather than to minimize them, and more often than not we feel guilty for things that we should never feel guilty about in the first place. For example, when I used to feel guilty because I'd spent a day worrying, there was really no logic to it. I wasn't guilty. I just *felt* guilty.

Here is one way to tell whether the guilt you are feeling is true guilt or false guilt.

1) **Did you actually do something that you believe is objectively wrong?**

If the answer is no, it's false guilt.

It the answer is yes, deal with it and then move on. Apologize, confess, make reparations if necessary, and deal with it. It may be tough to come to terms with it, but ultimately the freedom you will find at the other end of facing truth will be much more liberating than the prison of guilt. But once you've dealt with it, don't keep carrying the burden of guilt all your life. Guilt feelings that remain long after a situation has been resolved are false guilt, plain and simple.

2) **Have you confessed to whoever you needed to confess to, made reparations where necessary and faced consequences if necessary?**

If the answer is yes, the burden of guilt you continue to carry is false guilt because the real guilt has been dealt with. Your emotional pain receptors have made you aware that you needed to deal with a situation, and you have dealt with it. Now you need to learn to move on and leave the guilt behind.

Finally, try to remember that if you are struggling with depression you usually won't need to go any further than the first question above. More often than not, you're feeling guilty when you haven't actually even done anything objectively wrong. You're experiencing false guilt.

Maybe you're like me, stuck in a vicious cycle of false guilt. For years, I would feel guilty about something one day, feel guilty for feeling guilty the next day and then start feeling guilty for feeling guilty about feeling guilty.

Is there anything logical about that cycle? No. Absolutely not!

But it took me years to overcome it. Even after I realized it was false guilt, it took me awhile to retrain my brain to recognize those false guilt feelings as nothing more than what they were: symptoms of my depression.

You may not overcome false guilt overnight, but I challenge you to begin the journey of overcoming the lie of false guilt. Recognize today that guilt is not your identity. It's a symptom of your illness, and in most cases it is nothing more than an illusion. Fight that illusion with the truth that you are not guilty. If you need to get help from a counsellor, please do so. But don't let guilt control your life.

Guilty is *not* who you are.

Chapter 8
Excessive Self-Examination is a Killer

One of the ways in which I used to torture myself was in the art of self-examination. If I was feeling especially low one day, I would sit around desperately trying to figure out *why*. This was closely linked with the guilt cycle. After all, if I was feeling this low it must be my fault, right? However, it wasn't exclusively related to my feelings of false guilt. Sometimes I just wanted to know *why* I felt the way I did.

Of course, part of me thought that maybe if I could figure out what triggered my current depressive episode I could solve the problem and then feel better. However, it never worked that way. Instead, I worked myself up into deeper and deeper spirals of depression while I continually focused on myself and my problems.

I also engaged in this art of self-examination whenever I started to feel better! I would start thinking through my day and analyzing my thoughts until I found something to worry about or be upset over. And then I would fall right back into depression again.

There is a place for self-examination, particularly when sitting with a counsellor and trying to unravel the cobwebs in our brains. However, most of the time self-examination doesn't help us. It is a tool we use to push ourselves deeper into the pit of depression, devastation and self-pity. If you focus on yourself long enough, your mind will always find something to feel sorry for yourself about!

I remember one day while I was working in East Africa amongst the poor when I had a dream. It was a strange dream, but I never forgot it because it spoke deeply about what was going on in my self-conscious. I had obviously been working through some of these issues about false guilt, excessive self-examination, etc., but at this point I hadn't come to understand it yet. Strangely enough, it was largely through a dream that my mind finally started to make sense of it.

In my dream, I had a lot of guns slung around me. It was a weird feeling because I hate guns, but here I was with a whole arsenal of them. There was an old man standing in front of me, and I picked up one of the guns and fired it at him. It was empty.

I picked up another gun and fired it. Empty.

Another one. Empty.

Another one. Empty.

And this went on and on and on until I finally found a loaded gun. Then I woke up.

Usually dreams make no sense to me, and I tend to assume they often have more to do with what I ate the night before than anything either spiritual or insightful. However, in this particular case the dream spoke to me pointedly because suddenly I realized what I was doing.

Whenever I started to feel better, my mind would start racing. I would keep thinking and thinking and thinking until I finally found a loaded gun that would put me right back into my depression.

I learned that thinking too much about *me* is simply not the way to stop depression. I learned that it was much better to focus my mind on other things, to let my thinking go outside of myself to others. If I would think about how I could help other people or be an encouragement to those I loved, I found that a lot more effective than the art of navel-gazing.

Are you a champion of self-examination? Stop it, please! If you sit around looking inward, you will always find a loaded gun with which to shoot yourself In the foot, but that is of no help to anyone. Try to learn to turn your thinking outward.

Is there a cause you can turn your mind and energy to? Are there homeless people or lonely people or hurting people in your community you could lend a hand to? Are there ways you can turn your mind outward rather than inward?

For me, at least, learning to spend less time looking inward and more time looking outward into the world around me changed my life dramatically. Perhaps it could do the same for you too!

Chapter 9
Sometimes Faith Can Make Things Worse

If you are a Christian, you might want to go to a Christian counsellor. That is completely understandable as you are wanting to talk to somebody who shares your own worldview. Just because somebody shares your faith though does not necessarily guarantee that they understand depression. Before you let somebody give you counselling for depression, I believe it is incredibly important to find out first if they are qualified to help with this particular illness and also to find out what they believe about depression. Not all Christian leaders or counsellors believe depression is an illness, and as a result, regardless of their good intentions, some can potentially do more harm than good.

In particular, I've witnessed three approaches in the Christian community that are unhelpful.

1) **The faith is all you need approach**

There is a movement among some Christian churches that teaches that God will heal all of your illnesses instantly if you just have enough faith. This particular belief has been popularized by certain faith-healers on television, so most of the world is familiar with it. We've all seen the familiar picture of someone standing up from a wheelchair and proclaiming that they've been healed.

Now I'm not mocking faith or even making a comment at this time about whether or not God can heal. However, even if you believe that God does heal, there is no evidence that he *always* heals.

Kathryn Kuhlman, one of the first famous faith-healers in America in the last century, had a heart condition all her life that was never healed, and she died from a failed open-heart surgery in 1976. Does that mean that God never used her to heal people? I'm not saying that. This is not the time or the place to debate over whether or not God heals people, but the point I want to make here is that even if he does, it is only an immature faith that teaches that he *always* heals. Ultimately, everyone dies, and illness is a part of life.

I knew one young lady whose pastor told her that the reason she had depression was because she didn't have enough faith. Her whole church group eventually shunned her because they felt that her depression was a sign of her not being a genuine Christian. Needless to say, that church's approach toward depression was both dangerous and foolish.

Her church's immature faith taught her that depression wasn't the problem. Instead, she herself was the problem! This kind of teaching has led a lot of people to abandon church, and I am sure it has led people to the despair of a deeper depression. Tell a depressed person that they themselves are the problem, and you remove all hope from someone who is already in despair. There is nothing more dangerous than that!

If your church teaches you that your depression is a sign that you don't have enough faith, don't believe it! Their extremism is not biblical, not practical, not reasonable, and not true. And if you find yourself going to a counsellor who teaches you this, run!

2) The repentance is all you need approach

There is a famous Christian author by the name of Jay Adams who invented a method of Christian counselling he calls *nouthetic counselling.* The claim of this method is that it is all based on the Bible. To many Christians, it sounds like a great idea. What could be better than Bible-based counselling?

However, the problem is with his narrow interpretation of the Bible and the assumptions he makes about mental health, which by the way are not assumptions that come from either the Bible *or* the field of psychology! The underlying assumption is that sin is the cause of depression. If you are depressed, it's because there is an unconfessed sin in your life. The goal of this counselling approach is to help you to figure out what the sin is in your life that you need to deal with so that you can repent of it, change your behavior, and then be free from depression.

So basically, just as the first approach we looked at in this chapter says that a lack of faith is the problem, this approach basically says that the problem is that you are guilty. It plays right into one of the debilitating symptoms of depression and tells you that the voice in your head is right. Yes, you are guilty!

I am convinced that this is one of the most dangerous forms of counselling there is. Tell a depressed person that his depression is all his fault and you might as well just hold a gun to his head! If you are thinking of going to a counsellor who says he or she is offering biblical counselling, ask for more information. If they tell you they are offering *nouthetic* counselling, run!

This approach believes that the medical and psychological community are completely wrong about depression. To them, it's all about habitual sin and the need to repent. Any knowledge of how the human mind works or about chemical imbalances and other issues that effect depression are simply dismissed in favor of a simplified approach of attaching blame to the victim and leading him or her through a journey of trying to figure out "what they are doing wrong" to cause them to feel depressed.

When I was studying counselling in college, a friend of mine wrote a paper entitled something like, "10 Reasons Why Jay Adams is Wrong." It was a bold move because the professor who taught that particular class was a proponent of this kind of counselling and also a personal friend of Jay Adams himself. He reluctantly gave my friend a B+ when he obviously would have preferred to fail him altogether, but my friend was convinced it should have been an A.

He went to the teacher and told him, "I think this was an A paper. Why did you give me a B+?"

The teacher said, "Because I believe you are wrong."

My friend was angry and said, "I don't believe that even Jay Adams himself could answer the challenges in my paper!" He stormed off believing he had been treated unjustly.

Of course, most students would be happy with a B+, but my friend also happened to have an IQ of 180, a nearly photographic memory, and pretty much always got an A+ on all his work. Also, he believed as I do that this counselling approach is destructive and ridiculous, so he didn't like the idea that he'd received a lower mark than his paper deserves simply because the teacher disagreed with him.

However, the next day the teacher asked my friend if he could see his paper again. He showed him the paper, and the professor marked out the B+ and changed it to an A+. My friend asked, "What changed your mind?"

He answered, "I talked to Jay Adams. He couldn't answer any of your objections."

Dear reader, please do yourself a big favor. Stay far away from any pseudo-psychological approach that even it's founder can't justify when challenged with the facts. Don't go to someone who will try to make you think that it's all your fault. Find a real counsellor, not a fraud who wraps himself in the Bible like a wolf in sheep's clothing.

Do I sound like I have strong feelings about this particular approach? It's because I care about people who suffer, and I am convinced that this approach has caused greater suffering to many people. I'm not against people using the Bible, but this approach abuses it and is incredibly dangerous.

3) The Bible is all you need approach

In a way, both of the approaches we've already looked at here fall under this category. However, there are also other well-meaning approaches to Christian counselling that also fall under this umbrella. The idea is that psychology, science and medicine are irrelevant. Any truth that can be discovered is in the Bible, and if it isn't in the Bible it isn't of any use.

Would you want to go to a doctor who only uses the Bible to treat cancer or a broken leg and who dismisses medical science as irrelevant because it isn't described in detail in the Bible? I sincerely doubt it, and the same consideration should be in our minds when choosing someone to help with the illness of chronic depression!

I believe it is extremely important that if you decide to go to a Christian counsellor you find out what he or she believes about all this. A counsellor who dismisses all the knowledge available about the human mind and how it works will probably not be much help to you. That being said, there are plenty of Christian psychologists and counsellors out there who take an integrated approach. They use the Bible to comfort and encourage you, but they also use the vast knowledge that is available in the field of psychology to help.

Chapter 10
Sometimes Faith Can Help

A Muslim friend of mine from Syria celebrated Christmas with me this year. We didn't share the same beliefs about it, but we shared in friendship and respect, enjoying a delicious goose dinner and exchanging gifts. I also feasted with him after the fasting during Ramadan. I don't know about you, but I believe this is how adults should behave, with an attitude of mutual love and respect. At the places where our worldviews meet, we can share life together. In the areas where we believe differently, we can and should be able to respect one another. There is too much hate in the world to be adding to it, and if we shut each other out because of the things we disagree on we miss out on a wonderful opportunity of getting to know one another, learning from one another, and sharing together in the journey of life.

My personal world-view includes faith, and though I've warned about abuses of faith that can make depression worse, I do believe that it is also possible for faith to help. This is not a book created to try to convert people to my own worldview and I recognize that my readers include people of various faiths as well as those of no faith at all. Whatever your personal worldview, I am happy to hear about what you believe and what has helped you as well. Please feel free to find me on Facebook or contact me by email at nothingisimpossible.publishing@gmail.com and share your story with me. In this chapter I will share a little about my own understanding of faith, not to tell you that you must believe what I do, but simply as part of the sharing of my own journey.

I consider myself a follower of Jesus Christ as revealed in the Bible, and in my personal journey this has also helped me in the journey of recovering from depression. I haven't treated my faith as a magic pill expecting it to make me exempt from suffering or to take this thorn from my flesh in an instant, but I have found comfort, strength and help from it in my journey.

So for those who are interested, these are some of the ways I believe my own faith has helped me.

1) I had the support of a loving community

My church was supportive and helped to give me strength at a time when I really needed it. I know that not all churches do this, as I pointed out in the last chapter. However, I was fortunate in that mine was filled with caring and understanding people who never gave up on me.

I hope that you have people around you like that if you are struggling at this time. For you, it might not be a church. It might be family or work colleagues or fellow members of some other organization or club. It might be people with whom you gather for some other kind of religious group. It might even be people you gather with to talk *against* religion! But whatever shared belief or world-view holds you together, I encourage you to try to find a group of like-minded people who can encourage you and help give you strength when you need it most.

2) I never felt *completely* alone

Even in moments when I was in a severely depressed state and felt like nobody cared, I never believed for a moment that God had completely abandoned me. Something within me felt secure in the biblical promise that God would "never leave me nor forsake me."

For those who are reading this and thinking God is just some fairy tale, I respect your opinion. However, I have continued to believe that God was with me and could help me through this.

That doesn't mean that I didn't almost give up though. At one point, I very nearly did! However, I did believe that even when I could not pray, the Holy Spirit would pray for me in "groanings which cannot be uttered," that is that even in and through groans and tears he prayed and interceded for me and through me.

I also believed that God could give me strength when all my strength was gone. I admit that I did pray many times that he would take my depression away from me, and when he didn't I was disappointed. However, I found comfort in the words of St. Paul in 2 Corinthians 12. He said he had something he called a "thorn in the flesh." Nobody knows exactly what it was, but it was some kind of sickness or weakness that God did not heal or take away. Here is what he said about it:

> *Three times I pleaded with the Lord to take it away from me. But he said to me, "My grace is sufficient for you, for my power is made perfect in weakness." Therefore I will boast all the more gladly about my weaknesses, so that Christ's power may rest on me. That is why, for Christ's sake, I delight in weaknesses, in insults, in hardships, in persecutions, in difficulties. For when I am weak, then I am strong.*[v]

I was reminded that even in my weakness, God could give me strength. And I do believe that this belief helped me not to give up in the moments when everything else within me told me that I should.

3) **I believed that my guilt was taken care of**

Followers of Jesus believe that his death on the cross dealt with all our "sins," all the things we have done for which we have acquired guilt. We believe that when we trust him he forgives us of all the bad things we've done and somehow literally takes our guilt away.

There is a Bible verse that I memorized while in the depth of depression, and it helped me to reprogram my mind when my depression kept trying to tell me that I was guilty. The verse says this:

> Therefore, there is now no condemnation for those who are in Christ Jesus, **2** because through Christ Jesus the law of the Spirit who gives life has set you[a] free from the law of sin and death.[vi]

These two words, *no condemnation,* became an important part of my mental arsenal. I would often repeat them to myself whenever I was in the midst of trying to condemn myself!

Ironically, I know that a lot of Christians are champions of condemnation. They condemn others and each other, and they give Christianity a reputation amongst many as a judgmental group of people. However, those who actually follow the teachings of the New Testament cannot condemn. When they do, they actually deny the teachings of the Jesus they claim to follow and of the teachings of the New Testament.

True followers of Jesus have no right to judge others when they believe that God has forgiven them. There is simply no room for condemnation in a worldview that claims to be all about grace.

As you know if you've read the previous chapter, I don't mean by this that there is no such thing as real guilt. Sometimes people do bad things! However, I believe that God is their judge, not me, and that even he has done everything he could to make it possible that all their true guilt can be dealt with so that they can be free of its burden. The goal is grace and mercy, not judgement and condemnation.

I know a church in California where they live by the motto: "Jesus didn't condemn me, so I won't condemn you either." They are a very welcoming group of people, and in their midst you experience genuine love. We need more Christians like that, people who practice the love their Bible teaches.

I try my best to live by this motto and have done so for a long time. I try not to condemn people. Instead I try to find the best in them and to love them and accept them as they are.

However, for years I was pretty good at practicing this toward others but not toward myself. Somewhere along the way, I learned that I needed to be as forgiving toward myself as I try to be toward others. Learning to forgive myself has been an essential part of my recovery.

If you are a Christian, I encourage you to also learn these lessons. And if you're not a Christian and you believe the whole concept of faith is crazy, I still encourage you to glean this lesson from my words as they can be applied with or without believing in God:

Don't condemn. If you can learn not to condemn, it will set you free in many ways!

Many of us waste a lot of energy in condemning people, and really it hurts us more than it hurts anyone else. We fill our emotional reserves with pools of bitterness, and it poisons us inside and out. If we could learn to stop condemning people, including ourselves, I believe it would take a lot of the sting out of depression.

Depression feeds on our negative emotions. If we could learn to forgive others more easily, and to forgive ourselves, our depression would have a lot less to feed on.

Don't be quick to condemn others. Instead, look for the things you share in common in your humanity and try to find the common ground in which you can meet. As you do so, you may find friends in the most unexpected of places.

And then try to extend the same grace to yourself. If you can learn to forgive yourself and to stop condemning yourself, you may find friendship in an even more unexpected place: within your own heart. You might even learn to like yourself!

These are some of the lessons I have learned from my personal life of faith. I hope to hear your stories too and look forward to hearing from you!

Chapter 11
Weebles Wobble, But They Don't Fall Down

One important life-lesson I learned was from the story of a bird and a weeble. I heard the story when some of my friends and I decided to take a trip to Northern Ireland. One of my friends came from a town called Coleraine on the north coast, and we all went together to her old family home for a few days. It was in Coleraine, and then later in the footsteps of a giant, that I had a breakthrough.

We stayed in a big, cold house in the town. We ate dinner together and played games. There was an old television in the house, and we wanted to watch it, but my friend said we couldn't watch it because the house didn't have a television license. In the UK, you see, you're not legally allowed to watch television if you don't pay for a license. One of my American friends asked her, "What will happen if you watch TV without a license? Will anybody know?"

She said, "There's a wee man goes around in a van with a detector and he can tell if you're watching it."

"Really?" they asked. She just smiled and didn't give away if she really believed that or not. However, I have since lived in the UK long enough to know that many do, indeed, believe that the BBC has vans going around checking in this way. I don't know if it's true or just a myth, but I do know that one of my friends did later receive a letter at his apartment from the BBC saying that they knew he'd been watching TV without a license and that he would be fined if he didn't get one.

Whatever the case regarding "the wee man" in the van, however, we ended up spending our time there without television because the house didn't have a TV license. This led to a few days of being disconnected from media, which I do honestly think led to my mind being a bit more receptive to the stimuli in the real world around me.

On the first night, everyone but me stayed up late playing games, laughing and having a good time. However, I was feeling particularly depressed, so I went to bed early.

Then the next day, we all went to hear a speaker whom my Irish friend knew and respected. I don't remember the subject he spoke on, but I will never forget one story he told. It was a story about the bird.

He said he used to have a bird that he kept in a cage, and he was always giving it toys to play with. Unfortunately, the bird tore up every toy he gave it. But then one day, he got an idea. He decided to give the bird a toy it couldn't destroy.

He gave it a weeble.

Do you know what a weeble is?

Weebles were roly-poly toys created by Hasbro in the early 1970's. They were created with a basic egg shape. The top would be in the form of an animal, a person or some other thing. The bottom was rounded with a weight located in the bottom center to be lifted off the ground. You could knock the little weeble character down, but as soon as you did, the gravitational force would lift the whole weeble back up to an upright position.

Here's what happened to the bird. It became increasingly frustrated because it had never had a toy that fought back before! The bird would knock it down, but the weeble would just pop right back up. And the harder the bird attacked the toy, the harder it would come back up and hit the bird back. Eventually, the bird realized that it couldn't defeat the weeble, so it stopped trying to destroy it and learned to enjoy knocking it around carefully.

Now for some this story might raise questions of animal rights. The bird was in a cage, and the guy gave it a toy that kept hitting it back! However, on that day my mind was drawn to the imagery of the weeble.

In the early days when this toy was released, the advertisements used this slogan:

"Weebles wobble but they don't fall down."

Humanity is an awfully lot like the weeble. Humankind has been hit with so much tragedy, but it's resilient and keeps bouncing back. And I realized that I am like a weeble too! I may get knocked down, but the important thing is not about how often I get knocked down. What matters is the getting back up part of it!

No matter how many times we've been knocked down, and no matter how hard, it is never too late to get back up again. It may not always be easy, but it's not impossible. If we will develop a fighting spirit within us toward this horrible disease of depression, we may find that it can serve as a weight within us that reacts to the gravitational pull of life and lifts us back up to a standing position! The harder you hit the weeble, the harder it gets back up!

The next day, we all went to the Giant's Causeway. It's a fascinating spot on the northern coast of Northern Ireland, a true wonder of nature. It's an area of land beside the ocean covered by about 40,000 interlocking basalt stepping stones. In reality, it's the result of a volcanic eruption a very long time ago, but according to legend the columns, or stepping stones, were built by a giant from Gaelic mythology. He was challenged to a fight with a giant across the North Channel in Scotland and built the causeway across the channel so that the two giants could meet. On the Scottish side, there are identical columns on the Scottish isle of Staffa.

The columns really do look like stepping stones as you walk on top of them, and they are a fascinating thing to see. I wandered off by myself as I walked across the columns by the sea, and I found myself in a spot where it was just the steps, the sea and me. As the waves beat against the causeway and the breeze blew through my hair, I felt an incredible peace come upon me. I stood there and thought about the weeble, and suddenly found myself speaking out loud.

"I'm back," I said.

And then I went back home to Scotland and began my climb to freedom.

Chapter 12
Two Steps Forward, One Step Back

Emotional healing of any kind doesn't happen overnight. You don't just read a book or attend a seminar and walk away healed. You also don't usually see your whole world change after a new revelation. For example, that day on the Giant's Causeway was a turning point for me, but it wasn't the end of my struggle.

It takes time.

The same truth applies to the time when I finally got help from a qualified counsellor. That was another step forward for me, and my life was changed by revelations about false guilt.

But it didn't make my false guilt battle end overnight. I gathered new information about how my mind works and began to apply it, but it took me awhile to internalize it to such an extent that false guilt no longer ever controlled my mind.

I've learned that overcoming things in the emotional realm tends to be a journey, and the journey is not always one of taking steps forward every day. Sometimes there are relapses. However, I learned that relapses don't necessarily mean failure.

I learned that we move forward by taking two steps forward, one step back. And that's ok. It might be two steps forward, one step back, but it's still ultimately forward.

Think of it this way.

You are X, and you are trying to get from A to B:

AX-----------------B

When you first have a breakthrough, you take two giant steps forward.

A--X---------------B

It feels really good, and finally you start to think there is hope. You may even have a moment of elation in which you think you'll never be depressed again.

But then reality sets in. You have a really bad day, and you slip back into depression, or feelings of guilt, or whatever it is your mind and emotions are struggling with.

A-X----------------B

When this happens you probably feel like a failure. You say to yourself, "I thought I was finally getting somewhere! I thought I was overcoming this. I thought I had hope, but now I'm right back where I started."

But here's what you need to understand. You're not back where you started. You've taken a step back, but you're still on your way. The journey may have a lot of setbacks along the way, but it's still two steps forward, one step back. Ultimately you're still moving forward.

Get up. You can do this. Remember the lessons you learned in the better moments. You can keep moving forward even if sometimes it feels like you can't.

After you've had a bad day, or a bad week or whatever, you will manage to pick up and take another two steps forward.

A---X-------------B

Then another day you might take another step back.

A--X---------------B

It may feel like the progress is slow, and you may feel like you're starting all over again.

But you're not.

Two steps forward.

A----X-------------B

One step back.

A---X--------------B

Two steps forward.

A-----X------------B

One step back.

A----X-------------B

Two steps forward.

A------X-----------B

One step back.

A-----X------------B

A-------X----------B

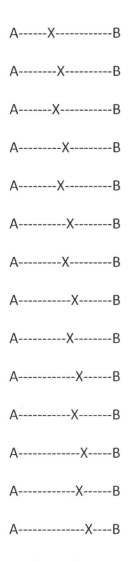

A------X-----------B

A--------X---------B

A------X----------B

A--------X--------B

A-------X---------B

A----------X-------B

A---------X--------B

A-----------X------B

A---------X-------B

A------------X-----B

A-----------X------B

A------------X----B

A-----------X------B

A-------------X----B

Until one day you will look back and be surprised at how far you have come!

It's a journey, but that's ok. In fact, to be honest, this may have been one of the most valuable lessons I have learned along the way. I learned to understand that even though I wasn't where I wanted to be yet, I wasn't where I used to be either. Day by day I was travelling toward a better life, toward more control over my thoughts and emotions, and one day I did look back and find myself amazed at how far I had come.

Have you experienced what you thought was a positive leap forward in your fight with depression only to find yourself feeling defeated again later? Do you feel like you were doing well but then ended up back at the start again?

Don't believe it! You are not back where you started. You may have taken a step back, but the backward steps are also part of the journey. I challenge you to believe that you can move forward again. You may need the help of professional counselling, as I did. You may need medical help, as I did also! But please find the help you need and don't give up.

Two steps forward, one step back.

But always forward.

You can do it!

Chapter 13
The Value of a Media Detox

Now I honestly don't know if following the example I'm sharing here would help you or harm you, but it helped me. One day I decided to take a complete media fast for a whole week, and it was an amazing experience.

I like watching television, I enjoy social media, and I use the internet every day. There is nothing wrong with these things. However, it did occur to me one day that our minds are constantly bombarded with stimuli, and I wondered what would happen if I gave my mind a "detox."

I was living in Mexico at the time, involved in a project that was helping people in a poor community in the state of Sonora. For one week, I didn't look at Facebook or Twitter or even check emails. I didn't turn on the television, and I didn't even read a book. I am an avid reader, so not reading a book was just as hard for me as not checking Facebook would be for many.

Now if you're thinking, "What did you possibly do with yourself for that whole week?," I completely understand your question! Most of us have become so dependent on media that it seems almost impossible to survive without it. In fact, there is even a new word in the English language that shows just how dependent we've become on technology and media.

"Nomophobia" is defined as "an irrational fear of being without mobile or cell phone contact." Some people literally panic if they lose their phone or lose reception because their cell phone has become almost a part of them. In case you're curious, by the way, the word was formed by a combination of the words no, mobile and phobia, and it is not in any way related to the similar word, "Gnomophobia," which is an irrational fear of garden gnomes!

However, I am happy to report that I didn't suffer from either nomophobia or gnomophobia during my media fast. I kept my mobile phone off the whole time, and I didn't actually see any garden gnomes.

So what did I do?

It turns out that a few things happened:

1) I found myself talking more to the people around me
2) I found myself *listening* more to the people around me
3) I noticed and appreciated things in my environment that I had never noticed or appreciated before
4) After a couple of days of initial nervousness, I felt a kind of peace I hadn't felt in a long time

Just as our diets tends to introduce a lot of toxins into our systems and can benefit from time to time from some sort of detox, I believe that our brains are also filled with the toxins of media stimuli.

Now I don't mean that all media is toxic or that it is bad. However, we do tend to be bombarded with messages about how we should think, what we should believe about ourselves and others, how we should look, act or dress, what we should buy, etc. And though many of these messages come to us subconsciously we start to internalize them. Sometimes they put pressures upon us, sometimes they anger or confuse us, and sometimes they just fill our minds so full that we have no space left to think about other things. Things like noticing, talking and listening to the people around us.

It may seem like a scary idea for someone who is depressed to be left alone with his or her thoughts. That's probably one reason why we tend to fill our lives with noise. However, for me at least, it was an incredible time of healing. I didn't spend it all naval gazing. If I had, I suspect it would have been more harmful than helpful. What I did, however, was fill my time with other things that proved healthy.

Another thing that a media fast can do for some people is lower their blood pressure or anxiety levels. A lot of people get caught up in fierce debates on Twitter or Facebook, and these debates tend to raise their anxiety levels through the roof. Here are some other ways that social media can increase anxiety in many people:

1) Unhealthy comparisons

People tend to post the best possible images of themselves on social media. We see their doctored-up Instagramed pictures from their tropical holidays in the sun, and suddenly our quiet morning alone reading a book in Starbucks or McDonalds just seems to pale in comparison. We forget that other people have struggles too when we see them constantly advertising what a "wonderful" life they have, and this can lead to a sense of self-consciousness. In the field of psychology, there is increasing evidence that this social-media induced self-consciousness often leads to perfectionism, which can often lead to anxiety disorders, and even pervasive thoughts that are indicative of things such as Obsessive Compulsive Disorder.

Another way in which social media can draw us into unhealthy comparisons is through the obsession it creates with "likes, retweets and shares." For many of us, whenever we post something, we find ourselves continually drawn back throughout the day to see how many likes or retweets we've collected. And if we see other people we know getting a lot more social media attention, we can actually begin to feel inferior, unnoticed or even unloved.

These feelings are irrational, but they are also pervasive. Our actual value is not dependent on how many likes we get on Facebook, and real love doesn't come through a computer or a phone screen. However, the more our minds are focused on these things, the more likely we are to become obsessed with them and to develop an unbalanced view of their importance.

A media fast can go a long way in helping us to break our dependence on these things and to clear our minds of the toxic beliefs we have developed about them.

2) An unhealthy fear of missing out

Mental health specialists are also noticing that people's minds often become obsessed with pictures they see of parties they weren't invited to, weddings they couldn't attend because of their busy schedules or for other reasons, and various events and experiences that they either don't have the time or the opportunity to share in. It's possible for many to find themselves spending more time feeling anxiety about things they are missing out on than noticing the things and people that are actually present in their lives in the real world. The irony is that they then might miss out on the things actually happening right around them!

3) An unhealthy addiction

A study done by the University of Chicago has determined that social media is more addictive than cigarettes and harder to give up than alcohol. Physically, our brains receive a dopamine high when we share, like and receive likes on social media. Dopamine is a chemical that's associated with pleasure, so the result is that this gives us a momentary feeling of happiness. Our bodies start to crave that feeling, and we find ourselves on what's called a "dopamine loop." We feel the need to keep coming back for more, and more, and more, and more...

Now at first glance, one might think that this is harmless. We may find ourselves obsessively seeking more pleasure, but what's wrong with pleasure? And on a surface level, I would agree. Pleasure can be a very good thing, obviously. However, the problem comes after the high is over.

When our social media experience doesn't give us enough dopamine "hits" or "likes" we can feel the loss deeply. Have you ever found yourself feeling more depressed when a picture or post you shared didn't get many likes or comments? This is part of the unhealthy side of social media addiction.

Now if we are addicted to something, it is clear that we will also suffer some kind of withdrawal when we quit "cold turkey." I experienced some of that when I had my media fast. In my case, however, I found myself seeking different ways to fulfil my need for pleasure. I found it by opening my eyes to the things and people around me, and for me it worked. Of course, the first couple of days were hard, but by the end of the week the effort of detoxing mentally proved very helpful for me.

As a word of caution, however, I want to reiterate that I don't know if this will work for everyone. If it resonates with you as something that is worth trying, I encourage you to give it a try. However, if it doesn't work, please don't allow perfectionist tendencies to lock you into the commitment if after a few days you find it is not helpful. As with any idea I share, take what works for you and toss aside what is different. We are all different. Our level of addiction can be different as well, and some people may need to taper off social media gradually for something like this as quitting "cold turkey" could actually prove traumatic for some!

Other ways you might consider applying this could include such suggestions as these:

A) Unplug once a week

Maybe a media fast for a whole week isn't practical for you, but what about choosing one day a week in which you leave your cell phone at home, turn off your computer and allow your mind to focus on other things? A regular practice such as this could prove very healing and helpful for many.

B) Stay away from specific triggers when you're struggling

For some, a complete media fast might not work, but you might need to unplug yourself from specific media during times in which you are struggling. For example, if you find that reading through people's stupid comments on Twitter makes you feel more anxious, maybe you need to take a day off of Twitter, or if you find that watching the news makes you feel depressed maybe you should switch off the news some nights and watch a comedy or something instead.

I've had some days lately when I was starting to feel anxiety because of people on Twitter sending me nasty messages or making disparaging comments, so now I occasionally take a Twitter-free day. Usually, I find that when I return the next day it doesn't bother me as much anymore.

C) Refuse to be drawn in

If you find that getting into social media arguments depresses you or increases your anxiety, you might need to consider ways of not allowing yourself to get drawn in to certain discussions. It's good to have an outlet to express ourselves, but sometimes the hostility we encounter on social media can be debilitating. When this happens, we need to figure out a way to make our social media experience into a healthier one.

In my case, I stopped sharing political opinions on Facebook. A lot of people I grew up with or whom I know personally are on my

Facebook, and I found that when people I knew attacked me mercilessly for having a different opinion than them I tended to sink into a deep depression. First, I would get angry, but then I would get depressed. My desire to be liked came into conflict with my desire to stand up for my convictions.

What worked for me may not work for you, but what I did was to move my political opinions to Twitter. Most of my friends and relatives don't even know how to find me on Twitter, so through that media I have found myself less personally affected by the opinions of cyber-bullies. I actually get attacked even more on Twitter than I did on Facebook, but as the attackers are all strangers I find that they usually don't effect me as much. When they do start to effect me, I take a step back for a day or two, but most of the time I just block them and move on. I don't know them, I have nothing invested in a relationship with them, so their opinions don't effect me the same way.

I've also talked with others on Twitter who have found that exact same move helpful. They stick to their funny cat videos on Facebook and refuse to get drawn into any debate there, and on Twitter they feel safe to express themselves.

This won't work for everyone though! Some people might really need to just not involve themselves in discussing controversial subjects at all. If you find that it effects you negatively, try to learn to stay away from those discussions. It's good to be able to express yourself, but it's also important to find avenues to express yourself that are healthy for you, not ones that are destructive.

I continue to take media breaks of various kinds from time to time, and I am grateful for the breath of fresh air that those breaks give me. That being said, of course, I just checked Twitter to see how many likes my latest post had before I wrote this last paragraph! Ultimately, it's all about balance though, and I live my life on the constant quest to find that right balance. I hope you can find it too!

Chapter 14
The Value of Exercise and Water

Thanks to my pharmacist friend in Scotland, I learned the value of two very natural remedies that played a big role in improving my mood and my health. The medication was necessary, and so were the counselling. However, we are complex, integrated beings, and it's usually a combination of things that effect us. Two natural things that helped change my life were exercise and water.

1) The value of exercise

Bill, my pharmacist friend, told me I should take a 30 minute walk every morning. I didn't understand at the time how that would help me, but he explained to me that when we exercise, a natural chemical called dopamine is released into our system and effects our mood. According to him, a 30 minute walk can have the equivalent effect of a dose of anti-depressants. Whether that exact correlation is medically proven or just his opinion I don't know, but I have learned that the principle is sound.

I have to admit that there were times in my journey with depression when I simply could not have gotten outside for a walk. I can personally testify that it is possible to be so depressed that even getting out of bed is difficult! However, after the antidepressants took effect I was then able to force myself out to try walking. The results were very positive indeed!

There was a wooded area on the edge of Kirkintilloch, the Scottish town where I lived at the time, that used to be the home of a mental asylum. The old buildings were going to rot, and walking through the woods surrounded by the derelict old stone buildings felt very much like walking through a ghost town or the scene of a horror movie. But it was also very peaceful and relaxing.

I wore earphones as I walked and listened to music, and I developed the habit of taking a brisk walk every morning. When I moved to a different location, I found new routes to walk, and whenever I travelled I walked around new surroundings and explored. These walks always lifted my mood and proved to be a very important part of my recovery.

I've read recently that even a 10 minute walk can improve your mood for 2 hours. I can personally attest to the value of exercise from my own experience! It really works!

I live in Germany now and don't have a car, so walking is now just a natural part of my life. I no longer take my half hour walk first thing in the morning, but getting to and from work, the grocery store, the train station and all the places I need to go requires me to walk more than a half hour every day. I have grown to enjoy walking, and it has improved my health both mentally and physically.

Do you get regular exercise? If not, I encourage you to give it a try if at all possible. It really does make a difference!

2) The value of water

The second natural lesson was more of a surprise for me. I already knew that exercise was important even if I didn't have the energy or desire to give it a try for awhile. However, I didn't know water could change my life too.

In addition to my depression, I was struggling with a severe lack of energy. During my college years, I often missed the first class of the day because I simply couldn't get out of bed. I also had times I couldn't get out of bed because I was depressed, but I found that sometimes even when I seemed fine emotionally I still had absolutely no energy. Whether that was directly related to my depression or separate from it, I don't know. I also don't know whether it had an influence on my depression. As they say, "Which came first? The chicken or the egg?"

However, whatever the case, my friends arranged an appointment for me with a specialist to explore my energy problem. I shared all my problems with him and he wrote me an unusual prescription...for water. He diagnosed me with chronic fatigue syndrome and told me that one treatment for it that he believed was sure to help me was water. He said I needed to drink two liters of water every day and that if I did my energy would go up and my moods would improve.

Was this man's diagnosis of chronic fatigue syndrome accurate? I actually have my doubts, especially as no other doctor I've met has seemed to agree with it. However, his treatment plan did have a dramatic effect upon me.

I once read a book about ways of improving our health that was written by a prominent doctor in which he made the same recommendation. I can no longer remember the name of the book or the doctor, but I remember his advice. His reasons were different than the specialist's, but his conclusions were the same. He said that most Americans and Europeans are always a little bit dehydrated and that living in a perpetual state of dehydration effects both our moods and our energy. He also recommended a minimum of two liters a day.

This little book I'm writing is admittedly not a medical book. It's a book about my own experiences and the things that helped me, and

I don't know all the medical ins and outs of this. Feel free to research it further if you have doubts about these conclusions or if you just want to know more. However, I can testify from my own experience that keeping myself well hydrated has helped me considerably, and on any given day if I forget to do so I feel the difference immediately as both my mood and my energy take a dip.

The journey to recovery involves a lot of different little steps as we gradually learn to reorganize our lives and change our lifestyles in healthy ways. I have found that a combination of lifestyle changes, counselling, and medical help have helped me considerably. It's not about finding one "magic pill" that fixes us. It's about finding the help we need to learn to rebuild and become a healthier version of ourselves. For me, water and exercise have been two of the helpful ingredients that have helped me along my way.

Chapter 15
The Value of Trying Something New

"It was a clear moonlit night. I heard the buzz of the planes first. Then I saw them flying over. Soon the horizon was lit up with fires as the bombs dropped."

George Renfrew was sitting in his chair with a banjo-ukulele in his lap as he shared these memories with me. As he talked, he looked as if these events from World War II were just as fresh to him as if they had happened yesterday.

Every week for a year, I traveled through the countryside of Western Scotland to teach this 87 (and later 88) year old man how to play a ukulele. The last part of the journey took place on a small single-track road that leads to his farmhouse, and whenever I arrived I knew that he would not be the only one who would be learning something that day.

At that time, I was giving banjo lessons in Glasgow and Falkirk, as well as in some other locations across West Scotland, and the way I made contact with most of my students was by advertising on a site called gumtree.com, which is the UK's largest website for local community classified advertising. It's kind of like Craigslist in the USA. One day, George's daughter contacted me through the advertisement and asked if I could teach her dad how to play the banjo.

I phoned George and arranged to meet him once a week for lessons. He lived over 40 miles from my house, but I was able to go by his place on a loop to another lesson that was outside Glasgow. The drive was also relaxing as it took me by the ocean, where I stopped each week to eat my sack lunch by the water.

The first time I arrived at George's house, I had a little trouble finding it. After twisting and turning through the single-track roads, I made my last turn and heard my Satnav announce, "You have arrived at your destination." I was sitting in front of a large old building in the middle of nowhere. I knocked on the door, but there seemed to be nobody around.

I phoned George, and he explained that that old building was where Satnavs always sent people, but it wasn't where he lived. His place was apparently just off the grid enough that the GPS system didn't know about it! He told me to keep driving down the single track road until I found his place on the left.

I came up to a house and was soon greeted by an 87 year old man and his dog. I carried my big banjo into his house ready to give him a banjo lesson, and he pulled out a very small instrument that looked a lot like a toy banjo. I had to look up the instrument on the internet to discover that it was actually something called a "banjolele," also known as a "banjo uke," which is a kind of banjo ukulele and is played like a ukulele.

He explained to me he had purchased this instrument because he wanted to start something new. I happily agreed to teach him, and the next week I came with a ukulele instead of my banjo.

After that, I spent an hour in this man's house every week for a year. He learned the ukulele. I learned about history and was also inspired by this old man who believed it's never too late to start something new.

After each lesson, he made me a coffee and shared stories about a Scotland of another day. He lived in the coastal town of Largs during World War II. Because he had rheumatic fever, he wasn't considered healthy enough to join the army, so he had to stay home while all of his friends went to fight. "Now all my mates are gone, and I'm still here," he says.

He witnessed the Clydebank blitz on the 13th and 14th of March, 1941. He saw the planes fly overhead and watched as the town of Clydebank went up in flames on the horizon.

He also met people from all around the world during the war. "I've never seen the world," he says, "but the world came to me." Largs was used as an important Allied headquarters, so he learned to know soldiers from literally around the world. He heard their stories, learned of their cultures, and in a small seaside Scottish town whole worlds were opened up to him.

He has filled notebooks with the histories of ThirdPart Holdings, West Kilbride, the farming area where he lives. The lives and stories of generations enliven those notebooks that are filled with his clear writing.

I would think of all the things this man has witnessed, worlds that have lived and died on his doorstep, as he would pick up his banjolele and play the latest song I had taught him. I was also reminded that, while we should celebrate and remember our histories, we should also never think that it's too late to start something new.

Whenever this man picked up his instrument, I saw him as a symbol of new beginnings. Some people think, "I'm too old now. I have missed my chance."

However, if this man can start something new at 87, perhaps we all can take the challenge to make a fresh start....at 47, 67, or 27....

Many people live their lives in the past. If they have a glorious past, they tell the stories of yesterday and look longingly back at days they can never recapture. If they have a past filled with regrets, they look back and feel sorry for themselves, convinced that it's too late to make something worthwhile of their lives.

However, as long as there is breath in our lungs, we have the opportunity to make a fresh start. George told stories of the past, but he didn't live in the past. He picked up his banjolele and did something new for today. Perhaps that is one of the reasons he was still healthy at his age. He didn't spend his days weighed down with yesterday.

Picking up a ukulele might not be the answer for you, but perhaps the 87 year old Scottish ukulele man can be an inspiration to you as he was for me. If you have good memories, be grateful for them. If you have bad memories, remember they are in your past. You are alive today! Do something for today...and for tomorrow. You're not dead yet! So get up and live!

Inspired by George's example, I have also continually sought out new things to try. Whether it be a new cuisine, a new skill or a new experience, I have learned that one great way to fight depression is to keep myself from either living in the past or wallowing in my today by trying something new.

Since I met George, I've learned to play a Latin American instrument called the charango and taken up a new language. What new thing could you try today?

Depending on where you are in your journey, I realize that this challenge can take different forms. If you are in the place where even getting out of bed is a challenge, trying something new could be something as simple as trying to get yourself to a new restaurant or maybe even just going for a walk. Or if you are a little further on the road to recovery, you might find that doing something more radical could make a huge difference on your mental health. Is there a language you'd like to learn? A course you'd like to take? An instrument you'd like to play? Or something else?

George taught me that it's never too late to try something new.

Chapter 16
The Importance of Language

Language is a funny thing.

As someone who loves learning and teaching languages, I've learned that new languages can be both exciting and dangerous. The slightest mistake can get you into big trouble!

For example, I know a man from Florida who doesn't know any Spanish. One day, he visited me in Scotland and was going to Spain after his visit to speak at a conference. As I speak Spanish, he asked if I would travel with him to interpret for him.

We had a great time together in the Barcelona area as he spoke each night at this conference, and while he was there he decided he wanted to learn a few Spanish words. One thing he told me he wanted to learn was how to say, "Excuse me!" He said he had a tendency to put his foot in his mouth, and he thought this would be a useful phrase, so I taught him to say, "Discúlpame."

He practiced his new word over and over again and waited for an opportunity to say it. His opportunity finally came one afternoon while we were eating lunch with a big group of locals around a large table. When the time was right, he spoke out loudly: "Escúpame," he said. Unfortunately, he had changed the word just enough so that instead of saying "excuse me," he was shouting, "Spit on me!" The people thought this was hilarious and continually went around pretending to spit the rest of the week.

I heard about another occasion while I was living in Peru in the mid-nineties. A Christian missionary was learning Spanish in the country and was asked one day to stand up in front of a local church and pray. He didn't feel like he was confident enough to preach yet, but he figured he could handle a prayer.

When it came time to pray, he intended to start by saying, "Let us pray." However, he unwittingly added a syllable, so instead he bowed his head solemnly and said, "Let us urinate!"

Yet another missionary in Peru was asked to preach at a Sunday service. He preached a sermon about a story Jesus told about a man who had a hundred sheep. One of the sheep ran away, and he left the ninety-nine sheep who were still in the pen and went to find the lost sheep. When he found it, he picked it up, threw it over his shoulder and ran home rejoicing all the way because he'd found the sheep that had been lost and now was found. The point of the story, according to Jesus, was that there is more rejoicing over one lost person who turns away from sin and follows him than over ninety-nine good people who have no need to repent.

However, this preacher got one word wrong in this Bible story. Instead of saying "oveja," which means *sheep*, he said "vieja," which means *old lady*. So instead of telling the story about sheep, he told it this way instead:

> Then Jesus told them this parable: "Suppose one of you has a hundred old ladies and loses one of them. Doesn't he leave the ninety-nine in the open country and go after the lost old lady until he finds her? And when he finds her, he joyfully puts her on his shoulders [6] and goes home. Then he calls his friends and neighbors together and says, 'Rejoice with me; I have found my lost old lady.'

The people politely listened while laughing inside and only told him what he had done afterwards!

I remember another time that language caused confusion in Africa. I was working with a team of volunteers in a rural area of Kenya, and we had been working in a village where everyone came from the Kamba tribe. In the Kamba language, they have an interesting tradition. Whenever an older person sees a younger person, he or she is supposed to say "wacha", which is a blessing. It kind of implies the idea, "May you be blessed to reach my age." The younger person received the blessing by saying, "a," which sounds basically like the English "ah."

We had a man named Mark who was working a lot with the children. He loved playing with kids, and the kids were always drawn to him. So he was accustomed to saying "wacha" a lot. That was good.

However, after we left the village we were travelling through rural Kenya on our way back to Nairobi and stopped at a gas station and restaurant for fuel and lunch. After we got out of the van, a large group of curious children came up to us. Mark was excited to see all the kids and decided to bless them immediately. He said, "Wacha."

They ran away.

Julius, a Kenyan friend who was part of our team, started laughing, and Mark asked him what happened. Julius explained, "These kids don't speak Kamba. They speak Swahili. In Swahili, *wacha* means 'leave.'"

Language is a funny thing! What you say one place can mean something entirely different somewhere else!

And of course it doesn't just happen when learning a different language. Even within English there are variations. For example, I got into trouble with a fellow American student one time while going to college in Scotland when I called her *ornery*. She got really upset at me and was hurt because she believed I was calling her bad tempered and difficult to deal with, while I thought I was just saying that she mischievous, but in a positive way.

How could we have had such completely different understanding of the same word? It turns out we were raised in different parts of America and with a completely different working definition of the word. My dad came from Oklahoma, as did the largest percentage of families in the town I grew up in, and I'm pretty sure the meaning of the word as I grew up with it came from that part of the country.

But here is what had caused the misunderstanding. I have since learned that my friend's definition is, indeed, the official definition of the word. It means, "difficult to deal with, bad-tempered or having an irritable disposition."

However, the definition I grew up with is basically, "a good-spirited trickster, a cute yet exasperating individual, or someone who is mischievous (with a positive connotation)" and we pronounced it "awnree" with two syllables, whereas my friend, who was from Michigan, pronounced it "ornery" with three syllables. My research later in life has shown that this is a minority definition of the word in common usage in certain parts of America, but it is not the dictionary definition that is used in other parts of the USA.

So even for two people who are from the same country and speak the same language, it's possible for misunderstandings to arise as a result of different understandings! A lot of linguistic misunderstandings are humorous as most of the above stories are, but sometimes they can also be painful when our words inadvertently cause pain as mine did with my American friend in Scotland.

The words we use have power. Words can make us laugh, and they can make us cry. Words can bring peace, and words can start wars.

Words have power, and it's the power of our words that I want to consider in this chapter. I've always known that words have power, but there's a lesson I learned about this that eventually played a big part in my recovery.

There's an ancient proverb that says, "The tongue has the power of life and death and those who love it will eat its fruit."[vii] Our words have the power to be life-giving and life-affirming, but they also have the power to drain life way, to be curses instead of blessings.

Another ancient text says, "Kind words and forgiveness are better than charity followed by insults."[viii] In other words, even if we do good actions, the good we do can be undone by unkind words because our words have great power either for good or for bad.

We tend to internalize the words we hear, especially when we hear them repeatedly. That's a psychological principle that advertisers have liberally taken advantage of. They know that if we hear the same thing repeated often enough, we unconsciously start to believe it, so they bombard us with repetitive advertising so that we will eventually feel compelled to buy their product.

If we hear something repeated often enough, we tend to start to believe it, and there's something about the way we are wired that tends to internalize negative things faster than positive things that are said about us.

Think about it: If somebody says five nice things to you and one negative thing, what will you remember? You'll probably obsess over the negative thing for the rest of the day!

For example, if somebody says to you, "You have really nice eyes! And I love your dress sense! I also love your sense of humor, and I admire your work as well! You have a nice smile too. Your hair could use a little work, but otherwise you look really great today!"

Be honest. Do you think you'd go away from that conversation feeling really good about somebody saying you had nice eyes and a nice smile? Or would you spend the rest of the day wondering, "What's wrong with my hair?"

I've often heard it said that for every negative thing we've been told about ourselves we need to hear seven positive things to balance it out. I don't know if that exact number is a verified scientific principle, but I do know that the general principle applies. It takes a lot of positive input to make up for the negative input our brains receive!

Knowing the power my words can have on other people, I've always tried to be careful how I talk to people. For most of my life, I've tried to make it a practice to say more positive and encouraging things to people than negative things and criticism, and when it is absolutely necessary to criticize I try to do so in the kindest and most constructive manner possible.

I remember hearing as a teenager that Amy Carmichael, a woman who lived most of her life rescuing children from temple prostitution in India, had a rule about speech in her community. She told everybody in her community that before they spoke they should ask themselves three questions before they spoke:

1) Is it kind?
2) Is it true?
3) Is it necessary?

Sometimes if I get upset I forget to follow this principle, but most of the time I try to run things I say through this filter. In this world a lot of unkind things are said unnecessarily to people, and they cause a lot of pain. I try not to add too much to that pain.

However, the lesson I learned in regards to my own mental health was that these principals don't just apply to the words we say to others. They also apply to the words we say about ourselves. If we put ourselves down a lot and speak negatively about ourselves, our minds internalize these negative words. They become a part of us!

I used to talk about my depression and my false-guilt cycle all the time. I didn't talk to many people about it, but I always had one or two people around whom I could trust. When I was feeling depressed, I would spend hours talking to those people about it. I would constantly seek reassurance, and I would repeat the same concerns and self-doubts over and over again.

Now don't misunderstand me. We do need to be able to talk about our feelings. Keeping everything bottled up inside can be just as dangerous, or even more so, than talking about them too much. Talking things through with a counsellor or a trusted friend can be a very healing experience.

However, the problem comes when we keep talking about it repeatedly. That's what I used to do. For example, I would get that feeling that I had "ruined the day," so I would talk my feelings over with someone I trusted. This was good. That person would listen and reassure me that my feelings were irrational and that I did not need to believe them, but then a few minutes later I would repeat the same concerns again and ask for more reassurance. I would then feel the need to talk to that person or someone else about the same things over and over again throughout the day.

And the feeling would never go away. Even when I received reassurance that it was my illness talking and not reality, I would actually find myself believing the voice of my depression more by the end of the day instead of less.

What was happening? My mind was internalizing my own words deeper and deeper the more I talked about it. The constant rehearsing of my grievance would deepen the grievance.

In more recent years, I have learned to take a different approach. If I feel an irrational thought taking root, I still talk to someone about it. However, once I've talked it through and see the irrationality of it, I determine to stop talking about it for the rest of the day.

Instead of constantly reminding myself to worry about it, I try to ignore that niggling voice within and talk about other things instead.

Since I have started doing that, I've realized that the lies begin to lose their power if we don't constantly justify them by repeating them over and over again! Our minds and hearts internalize the words they hear, even from our own lips, so we need to learn to speak positive things to ourselves.

I used to laugh when I heard self-help gurus telling people to memorize mantras and repeat them to themselves or listen to positive life-affirming statements on recordings over and over again. However, I have since come to understand the value of such things.

I never got self-help recordings or learned mantras personally, but I did follow the same basic principle. I learned life-affirming statements and repeated them to myself regularly, though I didn't find them from a self-help guru. I chose most of my statements from the Bible, though depending on your belief system and what inspires you, you may choose them from various sources, even movies or songs that have spoken into your life at some time or another.

Another things you might try is talking to people who know you well and asking *them* what are some good things about you that they see in you. Then maybe you should write those things down and start repeating those things to yourself until you start to believe them.

In my own very personalized journey, I found help from verses in the Bible that reminded me that there is no condemnation and all the wrong things I have done are forgiven and no longer exist. I continually reminded myself that I am not guilty. I also found statements that spoke positively of my identity as a human being and reminded myself that I was not a bad person and that the lies my depressive mind told me were contradicted by more positive truths.

The language we use affects the world around us. People are either encouraged by us or discouraged by us, and the reality is that our effect is seldom neutral. But the same is also true with the influence the words that come out of our mouths have upon our own psyche. I encourage you to think about what you talk about when you talk about yourself. Do you often put yourself down or rehearse grievances or negative things about yourself much more than necessary?

Be kind to yourself, and think about the effect your "self-talk" has upon your mind. Language is a funny thing. It is a powerful thing. And even the language we use about ourselves affects us deeply. For every negative thing you've said about yourself, try to think of seven positive things. It might be hard at first, but I promise you that they are there!

Chapter 17
The Importance of Getting Moving

You may not be a fan of the Bible, and changing your mind about that is not the purpose of this book. However, this is a book about my personal journey and experience in overcoming depression, and this particular lesson is one I came to understand through a story in the Bible. So in this chapter I will be sharing a story, not to try and convert you or beat you over the head with the Bible, but to share with you the example that helped me. Even if you don't believe that the Bible comes from God, you also might find wisdom in this story.

There's a story in the Old Testament about a guy called Elijah. According to the Bible, he was a great prophet who spoke on behalf of God to the nations. At this particular point in the story, which is found in 1 Kings 19, he has just experienced a massive victory in the chapter before. He would have been on an emotional high, similar to what you or I might feel if we had just completed an important project that had been exceptionally successful.

However, he'd also made some very powerful people very upset, particularly the king and queen of Israel. Ahab, the king, was a bad king but also a very weak one. However, his wife, Jezebel, was both powerful and evil, and she had vowed to have Elijah killed.

So now, though he had experienced a great victory, his victory was tainted by a sudden fear. He ran for his life and stopped somewhere in the desert under a broom tree. The story says, "He came to a broom tree, sat down under it and prayed that he might die. 'I have had enough, Lord, he said. 'Take my life; I am no better than my ancestors.' Then he lay down under a tree and fell asleep."[ix]

I read this story at a time when I was feeling particularly depressed, and I thought at this point, "Yes. That's me. I understand." Though he had recently experienced a major high, now he was utterly depressed. He despaired of life itself and just lay down and slept.

The story then says that an angel touched him and said, "Get up and eat." When he looked around, he saw somebody, the angel presumably, had left baked bread and a jar of water by his head. He ate and drank and then went back to sleep. Then later the angel came back a second time and told him, "Get up and eat, for the journey is too much for you." Once again there was food for him. He ate it and drank it and then, strengthened for the journey, travelled a long way to a place called Horeb.

This story seemed to show me a real understanding of depression. Nobody came to Elijah and said, "Just get over it!" Instead, he was given space to sleep and take some time to process whatever was going on inside of him. He was also told a couple times to get up and eat.

In my journey, this was important. Sometimes I needed to remind myself of the importance of getting up and eating something whether I felt like it or not. Diet is an important part of overcoming depression, though many of us may forget that. If we don't eat right, it effects our moods, and if we don't eat at all it makes us weak and feeds our depression.

So he had to be encouraged to get up and eat, and then he took a journey. But that's not the end of the story. The next part of the story is described as a dialogue between him and his God. It says, "And the word of the Lord came to him: 'What are you doing here, Elijah?'

"He replied, 'I have been very zealous for the Lord God Almighty. The Israelites have rejected your covenant, broken down your altars and put prophets to death with the sword. I am the only one left, and now they are trying to kill me too.'"[x]

Basically he was saying, "I have worked really hard, but I feel like my work is a failure, and now I'm all alone. And in addition to that, my life is in danger."

Other than the life is in danger part, I could identify with that too. When we are depressed we tend to see only the negative side of life, and we often feel like a failure. And the feeling that we are all alone and nobody cares or understands is Depression 101. That's what Elijah was going through. "Nobody cares, nobody understands, and I'm all alone."

How did God respond in the story? Well, this next part is a bit odd and seems to hold some metaphors and such that we won't try to dig too deeply into at the moment. It says God told him to stand on a mountain in the Lord's presence and told him that the Lord himself was about to pass by. Then as Elijah was standing on the mountain, a great and powerful wind tore the mountains apart and shattered the rocks, but it says the Lord was not in the wind. Then there was an earthquake and then a fire, but the Lord was not in those either. Finally after the fire there was a "gentle whisper,"[xi] and that's where God's presence was.

This isn't meant to be a Bible study, so I won't try to unpack the stuff about a powerful storm, an earthquake, a fire and then a gentle whisper here, except to say that in the context of depression the idea of a "gentle whisper" can be comforting. We don't need people coming in with powerful proclamations and hearty platitudes when we are feeling low. Sometimes we just need the presence of someone who gently reminds us that we are not alone and that somebody cares.

It's the next part of the story that really interested me though at the time. God had been really patient with Elijah. In fact, if you read the whole story you see that it didn't all take place in a day. It took place over a period of a month and a half. That's how long it took before God spoke to him in his last dialogue of the story.

That spoke to me too. It was a reminder that when dealing with depression sometimes we actually *need* some time to wallow. We can't always just "snap out of it," though some may wish we could. In this story, Elijah was allowed time to wallow and process before given the challenge. Then, and only then, was he given a challenge to move on to the next step.

Here's what happened next in the story. A voice, presumably God's, asked Elijah again what he was doing there and gave him a chance to voice his complaints again. Elijah repeated all his complaints again, and God listened. Then the Lord responded with the following words. I'll put them here and you can read them, but if they don't make much sense to you don't worry. I'll explain the context simply afterwards.

> The LORD said to him, "Go back the way you came, and go to the Desert of Damascus. When you get there, anoint Hazael king over Aram. Also, anoint Jehu son of Nimshi king over Israel, and anoint Elisha son of Shaphat from Abel Meholah to succeed you as prophet. Jehu will put to death any who escape the sword of Hazael, and Elisha will put to death any who escape the sword of Jehu. Yet I reserve seven thousand in Israel—all whose knees have not bowed down to Baal and whose mouths have not kissed him."[xii]

OK. Forget about all those names, and let's just get to the main point of what was happening here. God didn't respond with comforting words or platitudes. Now that he had given the man some time to rest, eat and deal with his thoughts, he basically said, "OK. Now it's time to get back to work. Get up and get moving." He gave him his next assignments and told him it was time to get moving.

He did, however, also give him one word of comfort. He told him that there were 7,000 others out there like him who had not given in to the enemy. He challenged his negative thinking with the facts: He was not alone.

So this is how this story helped me. It taught me a few life-lessons that I put into practice and which changed my life:

1) Sometimes I need time to wallow

First, it's ok to take some time to feel depressed, to lie down and get some sleep and deal with my thoughts. There is a time for that, and I don't need to feel guilty. To this day, I still allow myself some time for that if something big hits me and gets me down. However, the biggest point is that I can't let that time last too long. After I've taken a day to let myself process whatever pain I am enduring, I find I then need to get up and get moving.

2) It's important to get up and get moving

This is the big lesson really. If I'm feeling depressed, I can't allow myself to wallow in it too long. I also can't wait until I *feel* like getting up and getting moving. It is essential that I get moving whether I feel like it or not, and once I do I eventually will find that it helps.

Nowadays, I am doing really well. I am happy and enjoying life. However, I still have days when I wake up feeling depressed. At the phase of life where I am now, I realize that usually what that means is that I still need to get up and go to work. As I do, it helps. Sometimes as the day goes on, my mood changes and I begin to enjoy the day. Other times, I continue to feel low, but I function through the day and feel better the next day.

That, of course, is at the phase I am in now, one in which I have largely overcome the illness and feel that I am winning. You may not be there yet. If you are extremely depressed, getting up and going to work may be something that is simply impossible for you today. It won't be impossible forever though. No matter how hard it is for you to believe that right now, this is the truth.

However, getting up and getting moving is still something you may be able to start doing by taking baby steps. Start with something small. I know that just getting out of bed can seem like the biggest fight in your life, but try to get out of bed, take a shower and get dressed. If you can do more than that, try to get some exercise. As I mentioned in an earlier chapter, a pharmacist told me that 30 minutes of brisk walking has about the same effect on one's body as a dose of antidepressants due to the chemicals that are released with exercise. I don't know if that's scientifically proven, but I did discover when I was climbing out of the worst of my depression that if I could get myself moving and get 30 minutes of walking in each day it made a difference. And if you can't do 30 minutes at once, maybe you can start smaller. I am told that even a 10 minute walk can improve your mood for 2 hours, and my own experience would indicate that this is true.

What are some ways you can get moving today? I challenge you to make a start.

Part 4 -

Advice for People Who Love a Depressed Person

Chapter 18
How To Support A Depressed Loved-One

This chapter is especially for the friends and family of people who struggle with depression. If you love someone who is suffering, I am sure you want to help them. In this chapter, I want to offer you some advice as to things that might help you to be able to be of support to your loved-one.

1) Listen to us

Probably one of the best ways you can help us when we are depressed is to listen to us. We may say a lot of things that don't make sense because what's going on inside our heads may not always match what's going on in the outside world, but please listen when we tell you what we are feeling. The things we say in that state may not seem "real," but in that moment they are very real to us.

The temptation is often to try to talk us out of our depression, but we often can't be talked out of it. Sometimes what we really need is for someone to understand us. It can be really frustrating to sense that nobody understands or to have people constantly telling us how silly our thinking is. We know that our thinking isn't always rational when we are depressed, but it honestly doesn't help us to constantly be told that.

Sometimes we just need somebody to listen.

2) Don't say, "Snap out of it"

The temptation to say, "It's a lovely day outside. Let's enjoy it! Snap out of it!" can be overwhelming for someone who has never experienced real depression. You may be thinking, "But you don't have anything to be sad about. Things are going good right now."

The problem is that we already know that. Sometimes we might feel depressed when there is no recognizable outward reason for us to feel that way, and we may already feel frustrated about that. The problem is that we are not depressed just because of how well or badly our current situation is going.

Depression is an illness.

If someone had a broken leg, I am sure you wouldn't say, "Just snap out of it and go on a run with me." The problem with depression is that you can't see it as clearly as you can see a broken leg, but it's still just as real as one. When someone is depressed, he or she can't just snap out of it any easier than someone with a broken leg can get up and go for a run.

I mentioned in an earlier chapter that a doctor once told me to "see it through bravely." Basically, he was telling me I just needed to snap out of it, to pick myself up and just keep going. His advice was well-meaning, but it made me almost suicidal because seeing it through bravely or just snapping out of it was something I was completely incapable of doing. When he told me that, it made me feel helpless. It made me feel like I *should* be able to snap out of it, and I was all the more frustrated that I couldn't.

Depression is not just a bad mood. It's a sickness, and overcoming it simply doesn't happen overnight. We need understanding and patience.

3) Don't say, "I understand because I've had bad days too."

I've had people say this to me. "I've had bad days too. I understand exactly how you're feeling." However, once I talked it through with them I discovered that they really have just had "bad days." They've been discouraged, but they've never been depressed.

Discouragement happens when something we hope for doesn't happen or we aren't able to achieve something we'd hoped for. It can be pretty debilitating. However, it's a temporary condition. It's something that a lot of people can actually "snap out of," while others have to go through a process in order to overcome it.

For example, a man loses his job. He's put all of his hope into his career, and one day it's all taken away from him. The feelings he experiences may have a lot in common with depression, and in some cases a person in this circumstance may spiral into an actual depression. However, for others it's a bit different.

The biggest difference between depression and discouragement is that you get over discouragement. It may take time, but usually you move on from the circumstance that discouraged you and find hope and joy in something new.

The danger in equating discouragement or "a bad day" with depression is that it fosters the idea that you should be able to get over it. There definitely is hope for overcoming depression, but it's more complicated than that. Having experienced discouragement may indeed give you the ability to have a little more sympathy for us, but please don't think that it means you know what it's like because misunderstanding that can lead to a misunderstanding as to how it should be treated because the things that cure discouragement don't usually cure depression.

Treating depression like mere discouragement is kind of like giving cold medicine to a cancer patient. They are different problems, so the treatment plans are different.

4) Don't say, "You shouldn't feel that way."

This one is closely linked to the "snap out of it" issue. We don't feel this way because we want to. There's this heaviness upon us that we often can't explain, and when we are depressed we already know that this is not how we *want* to feel. However, when people tell us that we *shouldn't* feel the way we do, this plays right into the guilt aspect of the disease that many of us struggle with.

When you say, "You shouldn't feel this way," this is how my mind would have interpreted those words during the worst times of my depression:

    a) I am wrong to feel this way
    b) I am trying not to feel this way
    c) I am not able to change how I feel
    d) Now I feel guilty for feeling this way
    e) So now I'm even more depressed

Again, the good intentions are appreciated, but this just isn't helpful.

5) Don't try to fix us

I'm a fixer. When I see a problem, I want to fix it. However, some things are not easily fixed.

I'll never forget the time I tried to fix an old computer. It had slowed down and wasn't working right. It also seemed to be running out of space, so whenever I tried to save a file it would say there was no room on the hard drive.

I looked online for answers to my problem and found several things I could try. However, each thing I did made it worse! Eventually, I had to take my computer to someone who knew more about computers and get him to sort it out.

I also tried to fix a broken pipe once and ended up with a bigger leak.

Sometimes, you see, we're really better off calling someone in who knows more than we do about something because our efforts to fix things can actually make matters worse if we don't know what we are doing.

When it comes to depression, there really are way too many amateur counsellors in the world, people who think they can fix it but who know nothing about the disease. It's very important to realize that it's not something you can fix overnight. What we need from you is support, and one way you can support us is to accept that you may not have all the answers and that that is ok.

6) Be patient with us

Sadly, sometimes people give up on their depressed loved ones. Sometimes they take it personally when their loved one doesn't show the appreciation they deserve. Other times they get annoyed when their loved one goes through a vicious cycle and keeps repeating the same irrational thoughts. And sometimes they just find the pressure of living with someone who is depressed to be too much.

However, I want you to know that what many of us need more than anything is to know that somebody cares and will not give up on us no matter what. Is someone you love struggling? Do you love that person enough to not give up on him or her? If you'd give that person the gift of unconditional love, it really could change his or her life. It may not seem like they appreciate it right now, but if you'll hang in there I believe that one day you will see that it is worth it and that you will have given them some of the strength they needed in order to survive.

Years ago, somebody that I cared about was suffering from severe mental health issues, and unfortunately most of the people he knew gave up on him. Even his marriage fell apart. I had grown up with his wife, so many people would probably have expected me to cut him off in support of his wife. However, I chose not to take sides in their issues and just love them both. I felt it was important to let him know that I would never give up on him no matter what. I gave him a card with my assurances that I would always be there no matter what. There were times when he didn't feel like talking to me, but he knew I was there.

A couple of years later, his marriage was healed and he and his wife got back together. To this day, they are strong together, and he has overcome a lot of his mental health issues. He still struggles, but overall he is doing the best he ever has. And we are still friends.

Patience can be hard because the truth is that loving a depressed person can be hard on the person who cares for them too. However, if you love your loved-one enough to not give up, your love could really be the gift of life. It might even literally save their life one day.

7) Learn about depression

There are so many misunderstandings about depression in society, and one of the hardest things for us when we are depressed is knowing that so many people simply can't understand us. I encourage you to learn as much as you can about depression. Ask your loved one if they have any readings or videos you can read or watch that might help you to better understand their situation, and seek out opportunities to learn about this disease.

It's often said that nobody can fully understand a depressed person unless they have been depressed themselves, and of course there is a lot of truth to that. This is the case with any life experience. Nobody fully understands what a cancer patient goes through either, or an accident victim, or a rape victim, or anyone who is going through a traumatic life experience. It doesn't mean, however, that you can't learn as much as possible about your loved-one's situation so that you can give as much support as possible.

And of course one of the best ways to seek understanding is to keep going back to point number 1. Listen to us. Ask questions. Give us a chance to explain to you what we are feeling, and no matter how irrational our thoughts may sound on days when we are in the depth of depression, please don't laugh at us or judge us. Listen, and seek to understand us better.

8) Encourage us to get help

When we are depressed, we are sometimes our worst enemies. For whatever reason, we might resist getting the help we need. If you've read this whole book, you'll have seen that I resisted accepting medication first and later resisted counselling. In my case, I had misunderstandings about what medication and counselling meant, and I needed help in overcoming my misunderstandings about them before I was willing to try them.

For others, there can be a variety of reasons why they might resist getting help. In fact, some may simply feel so depressed that they can't find the motivation to get out of bed and go see a counsellor or get medical help when needed. Please lovingly encourage your loved-one to get the help that they need. Even if they resist to start with, they will probably thank you later.

9) Get help for yourself too if you need it

As I already mentioned, dealing with depression can be a challenge for the person who cares for the depressed person too. A lot of people forget about that. They focus on the one who is ill, but they forget that any severe illness takes a toll on the caregiver too.

If you are struggling while trying to encourage and help your loved-one, please don't hesitate to seek out support for yourself as well. It doesn't mean you're weak. It just means that you're human!

One way you might seek out support is to find a support group. Do you know other people who are caring for depressed loved ones? It might be helpful to meet up once in awhile and talk out your own concerns and difficulties. Having support from people who are undergoing the same experience can be incredibly helpful.

You might also find it helpful to get some counselling for yourself as well. A good counsellor can help you both in coping with your own feelings and with your questions about how to best support your loved-one.

You might even struggle with feelings of resentment. Maybe you sometimes feel like dealing with your loved-one's depression is robbing you of your own chance to enjoy life in some way. That's an understandable emotion, and you may be surprised to learn that it is common. Finding support from other people in the same situation as you, or from a trained counsellor, can help you to work through your own feelings.

And don't feel guilty for admitting that you need help too! If you are going to be a support to someone who is ill, it's important for you to be healthy too. If you need help, get help!

Depression is a common and debilitating illness. If someone you love is suffering and you are reading this today, I want to sincerely thank you for caring enough to read my words. It means that you are already trying to understand. Please be patient with your loved-one and don't give up on them. There is hope.

I've largely overcome my depression. I am living a fully functional, productive and happy life now! I hope, believe and pray that the person you love will one day be able to say the same thing about his or her life!

PART 5 -
A Closing Thought

A Final Word
There is Hope

Whether you are depressed or someone you love is depressed, one of the hardest things about depression is that it is easy to give up hope. When we're depressed, we often feel like there is no hope at all. We are stuck in a dark tunnel, and we become convinced that we will never get out of it into the light.

I remember feeling that way. It was the most difficult thing I have ever experienced. I felt utterly devoid of hope and truly believed that I could never be happy again. The heaviness upon my soul was so intense that I almost completely gave up.

However, I am so glad today that I did not give up! I love my life, and I am grateful every day that I didn't give my life up while I was stuck in that wretched tunnel.

There is hope.

If you are in that darkest place today, it may be really hard to believe, but it's still true. An old proverb tells us that "the darkest hour means dawn in just in sight." While in the midst of that darkest hour it's possible that nothing anybody can say will convince you that this is true, but I've experienced that darkest hour and come out to see the dawn.

Don't give up.

The sun will shine again.

About the author

Chris Lewis was born in Reedley, California. He grew up in the Lewis Family, a Christian family music group, and then later moved to Scotland where he went to university and then devoted much of his life to working with the poor and disenfranchised. In recent years, he worked in refugee camps in Central Europe during the Syrian refugee crisis. He currently lives in Germany with his wife, Karen.

Notes

[i] World Health Organization Website,
http://www.who.int/mediacentre/factsheets/fs369/en/
[ii] Lyrics, Belloc, Dan; Douglas, Lew; Parman, Cliff; and Levere, Frank, *Pretend*, 1952
[iii] Lyrics, Turner, John & Parson, Geoggrey, *Smile*, 1954
[iv] Dickens, Charles, *A Tale of Two Cities* (Oxford: Oxford University Press, 1950), Pg. 1
[v] 2 Corinthians 12:8-10
[vi] Romans 8:1
[vii] Proverbs 18:21
[viii] Surah 2:238, Translator, Itani, Talal, *Quran: English Translation* (ClearQuran, Creative Commons License)
[ix] 1 Kings 19:4-5
[x] 1 Kings 19:9-10
[xi] 1 Kings 19:12
[xii] 1 Kings 19:15-18

Printed in Great Britain
by Amazon

19998558R00079